Memory and Storage

TIME
LIFE ®

Other Publications:
WEIGHT WATCHERS® SMART CHOICE RECIPE COLLECTION
TRUE CRIME
THE AMERICAN INDIANS
THE ART OF WOODWORKING
LOST CIVILIZATIONS
ECHOES OF GLORY
THE NEW FACE OF WAR
HOW THINGS WORK
WINGS OF WAR
CREATIVE EVERYDAY COOKING
COLLECTOR'S LIBRARY OF THE UNKNOWN
CLASSICS OF WORLD WAR II
TIME-LIFE LIBRARY OF CURIOUS AND UNUSUAL FACTS
AMERICAN COUNTRY
VOYAGE THROUGH THE UNIVERSE
THE THIRD REICH
THE TIME-LIFE GARDENER'S GUIDE
MYSTERIES OF THE UNKNOWN
TIME FRAME
FIX IT YOURSELF
FITNESS, HEALTH & NUTRITION
SUCCESSFUL PARENTING
HEALTHY HOME COOKING
LIBRARY OF NATIONS
THE ENCHANTED WORLD
THE KODAK LIBRARY OF CREATIVE PHOTOGRAPHY
GREAT MEALS IN MINUTES
THE CIVIL WAR
PLANET EARTH
COLLECTOR'S LIBRARY OF THE CIVIL WAR
THE EPIC OF FLIGHT
THE GOOD COOK
WORLD WAR II
HOME REPAIR AND IMPROVEMENT
THE OLD WEST

This volume is one of a series that examines
various aspects of computer technology and
the role computers play in modern life.

UNDERSTANDING COMPUTERS

Memory and Storage

BY THE EDITORS OF TIME-LIFE BOOKS

TIME-LIFE BOOKS, ALEXANDRIA, VIRGINIA

Contents

The Power of Recall

Next to the speed with which a computer can perform its basic functions—adding, subtracting, multiplying, dividing, and comparing one value with another—no measure of such a machine's potential is more revealing than its capacity for storing, and recalling on cue, information and the instructions for handling it. Without the ability to squirrel away data and programs, a computer would not deserve the name. Like the simplest electronic calculator, it could handle only two numbers and one operation at a time, an unacceptable limitation for any but the simplest of data-processing tasks.

Computers store information and programs by means that are, in essence, either electronic or mechanical. Electronic methods, generally called memory, are highly valued for their ability to keep pace with the computer's central processing unit, or CPU, which typically shuttles bits of information and program instructions in and out of memory several million times a second. Because these electronic circuits are expensive and because the most common varieties lose their contents when power to the computer is interrupted for even a split second, the role of memory is that of a temporary niche for data and instructions that must flow quickly in and out of the CPU.

The memories of computers that were constructed during the early part of the 1940s rarely exceeded a handful or two of bytes, a unit of measurement equal to eight bits, or binary digits. (In their formative years, computers often handled bits—the basic on-off currency of their circuits—one at a time. It is common nowadays for a computer to work with groups of bits—known as words—of two, four, and even eight bytes, a feature that by itself can increase the speed of a computer many times over.)

Memory grew slowly, taking until the mid-1960s to pass the megabyte (one-million-byte) mark, but the advent in the 1960s of integrated-circuit chips—microscopic assemblages of transistors and other electronic components—brought with it a tremendous increase in the memory capacity of computers. Today, even the most unpretentious desktop computer may contain a million bytes of memory and have the potential for controlling several million more. Some supercomputers have access to more than four gigabytes of memory—or four billion bytes.

Nonetheless, it is almost an axiom in the world of computers that there is never available a satisfactory amount of memory. Programs and data tend to grow, first to fill and then to exceed whatever memory a computer may command. To handle the overflow, mechanical methods are brought to bear. Commonly called storage, these devices once retained information in the form of holes punched in paper tape or cards. After decades of applied ingenuity, holes have been supplanted by infinitesimally small regions of magnetism on recording tape and related media or by microscopic, light-scattering bumps embossed in a compact disk—the same kind of silvery platter that has brought such an uncanny realism to the reproduction of music.

7

Storage devices for computers are mechanical in the sense that retrieving a parcel of magnetically or optically stored information requires the use of machinery such as tape recorders and disk players in order to locate the data and convert it into pulses of electricity acceptable to the computer's memory and CPU. A reversal of the process is necessary to find unused space for storing the information and to record it there.

As rapidly as these mechanical processes may occur, storage devices at their fastest are many times slower than the purely electronic circuits of memory. Yet in a wide range of applications, this limitation is more than compensated for by the huge capacity of the devices, available at a small fraction of memory's cost per word. A further advantage of storage is permanence. Data committed to magnetic tape, for example, or to a compact disk will be retained for many years. Such media are ideal for archiving records that may be vitally important, though rarely consulted.

Storage has always been a relatively plentiful commodity. As early as 1890, the census of the entire United States was represented as holes punched in cards about the size of a dollar bill, and there was one for each of the nation's inhabitants. Had anyone wished to attempt the feat, details about the entire world's population could have been recorded in the same manner. There was virtually no limit to the amount of storage available.

The tabulating and sorting machines that were used to tally responses to that *fin de siècle* survey of the nation had no memory at all, unless the dials that showed totals could be classed as such. More than five decades later, computer scientists striving to develop a satisfactory memory would invent curious strains of electronic exotica: glass tubes filled with mercury, television-like devices flecked with luminous blips that represented data, and tiny doughnuts, or cores, of an easily magnetized iron alloy suspended at the intersections in a grid of fine wires. The last, called magnetic core memory, would find the widest use. Its ascendancy would spark a fierce battle to patent and market the technology and would pit the emerging computer giant, IBM, against three men who claimed credit for the invention.

HOBBLED BY WIRES AND SWITCHES

Perfecting an economical method for expanding memory was a matter of considerable urgency to pioneer computer scientists, as demonstrated by ENIAC, the first electronic digital computer. Assembled at the University of Pennsylvania's Moore School of Electrical Engineering between 1943 and 1945, ENIAC's purpose was to calculate trajectories of artillery shells. From this data were constructed aiming tables for use by American artillerymen. To program the machine, an operator had to set hundreds of switches and link various parts of the computer with a spaghettilike skein of cables, a chore that might take days to complete. This wires-and-switches approach to telling the computer what to do was so unwieldy that it discouraged the machine's use for solving a wider variety of problems.

Other computers of that era replaced ENIAC's wires and switches with programming obstacles of a different kind. Their programs were stored as holes punched in a paper tape, its ends pasted together to form a closed loop. A tape reader, which was connected to the computer, translated the holes into instructions for the CPU. Compared with the method that used wires and switches, programs that were stored on tape speeded the adaptation of a computer from one purpose to another; revising the machine's marching orders required nothing more complicated than changing tapes. But there was a cost. Access time, the interval needed for a computer to read an instruction from the tape, was so long that the CPU often spent more time waiting for commands than it did executing them. Part of the problem lay in the slow speed at which tape readers operated. Perhaps even more important was the fact that access to the instructions usually was serial in nature. After executing a command, a computer could move only to the next instruction on the tape, even when some other operation might be more appropriate for conditions that arose during the computations. No provision was made for random, or direct, access to the program—that is, for skipping directly to the next useful instruction.

From these experiences emerged a concept of memory that endures to this day. First, it should be erasable—one set of data or programs stored there should be easy to replace with another. It should be reliable, not inclined to erase or rearrange itself. Fast access was just as crucial; memory must not delay the computer's CPU. Furthermore, memory should be inexpensive, something that any computer could have plenty of.

As World War II drew to a close, a computer memory that satisfied these requirements remained elusive. The few half-promising candidates would all suffer, in one way or another, from overlong access times. An example was the electromechanical relay. In essence, this was a device consisting of a small iron bar that was wound with a coil of wire. When current flowed through the wire, it magnetized the bar, which then snapped open a spring-loaded switch. When the current was shut off, the iron bar was demagnetized and the spring snapped the switch closed. The relay's alternate positions—open and closed—could symbolize ones and zeros, the binary vocabulary of a computer. Though substantially quicker than paper tape, a relay's mechanical switch was still much slower than the electronic switches that made up a CPU, so this approach to memory was soon abandoned.

INTENTIONAL DELAYS
The next significant advance in computer memory was an American brainchild, the acoustic delay line. Developed at Bell Labs in the early 1940s by William Shockley, later to share a Nobel Prize for the invention of the transistor, the acoustic delay line stored binary numbers as sound waves. Numbers representing either data or instructions to the computer were held in the delay line until needed for processing by the CPU.

Typically, a delay line consisted of a glass tube, filled with mercury and plugged at each end with a quartz crystal. Electrical pulses representing bits of data or program instructions to be stored in the memory were fed to the crystal at one end of the tube, causing the quartz to vibrate in response. The resulting sound waves advanced through the mercury to the quartz crystal at the other end of the tube, causing it to vibrate in turn and reconvert the data into electrical pulses, which could be rerouted indefinitely through the mercury until the computer required them for processing.

As sound, the bits passed through the mercury 200,000 times more slowly than they zipped along wires as pulses of electricity. Thus, a tube a couple of yards long delayed—or stored—the bit stream for about one thousandth of a second, a lengthy period compared with the speed of a CPU, which could execute a thousand instructions during the same interval.

Although access to data stored in an acoustic delay line was speedier than what had been provided by the electromechanical relays it replaced, this kind of memory exhibited certain objectionable traits. For example, the bit stream's trip through the mercury could not be interrupted. Once the sound waves had begun their passage, the data that they represented could be retrieved only after it had crawled the full length of the tube. Moreover, the very nature of the delay line made it a serial device: There was simply no possibility of random access to data or programs stored there.

A CLIMATE-CONTROLLED MEMORY

Delay lines were also sensitive to the weather. Because the speed of sound in mercury is higher at cool temperatures than at warm ones, sound waves traveling through a delay line tended to accelerate or slow down in response to fluctuations in the ambient temperature. A change as small as one degree caused the computer, which expected data to exit from a tube punctually and at a prescribed rate, to misread the information. The result was loss or misinterpretation of data and program instructions.

Engineers attempted to solve the problem by isolating the delay line in a warm oven to stabilize the temperature of the mercury. Doing so, however, required an exasperatingly long warm-up period each time the computer was turned on. Other, less temperature-sensitive fluids—and even solid quartz—were tested as substitutes for mercury. The British computing pioneer Alan Turing suggested that, based on his theoretical studies of alcohol-and-water mixtures, the ideal delay-line medium would be gin. Unfortunately, the lower density of such materials reduced their ability to retard sound waves, so they saw only the most limited use for computer memory.

It fell to Herman Lukoff, a twenty-three-year-old research engineer at the University of Pennsylvania's Moore School, to overcome mercury's temperature-related handicap. For a computer called EDVAC, designed in 1945 by a team of engineers at the school, Lukoff devised a special package of electronics called a temperature compensator. His invention expanded or condensed the spacing between pulses in the bit stream en route to the delay line according to the temperature of the mercury in the tube. Doing so guaranteed that the sound wave associated with each pulse of data arrived at the end of the tube on schedule, regardless of how warm or cool the mercury might become.

By March 1947 Lukoff was ready to display his system at a convention sponsored by the Institute of Radio Engineers in New York City. No sooner had Lukoff begun his demonstration, however, than the mercury exhibited extraneous pulses that garbled the data stored there. The mystery pulses continued to course through the delay line every two seconds until Lukoff spotted the source of the trouble—a rotating radar antenna in the exhibit booth of the Army Signal Corps on the far side of the convention hall. The radar beam had struck the delay line with each turn of the antenna, triggering random pulses in the memory's circuitry. The army obligingly turned off the radar beam, and the new memory

Early Memory Workhorses

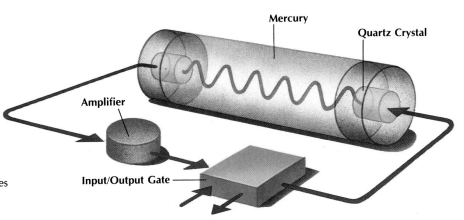

Acoustic delay line. This system, the first computer memory to see widespread use, was invented in the late 1940s. Electrical pulses, representing binary digits from the computer's central processing unit (CPU), are fed through an input/output gate to a quartz crystal, causing it to vibrate. The crystal's oscillations convert the pulses into sound waves that move along a column of mercury to another quartz crystal, which transmutes them into electrical pulses. After amplification, the data can be returned to the CPU for processing or sent on another circuit of the delay line.

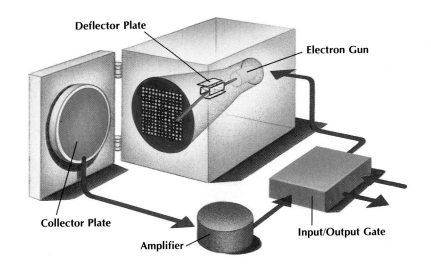

Williams tube. In this scheme, a cathode-ray tube (CRT) uses electrostatic charges to store binary data. A burst of electrons, emitted by a gun at the rear of the tube, is directed by computer-controlled deflector plates to predetermined spots on the CRT screen, where the burst leaves either a charged dot or dash. Because the charge dissipates quickly, the beam must re-create the dots and dashes five times each second. To retrieve data from memory, a metallic screen called a collector plate, positioned against the face of the tube, converts dots and dashes into electric pulses. They are amplified and returned through an input/output gate to the computer.

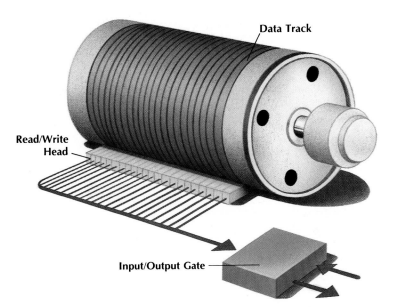

Magnetic drum. This device, invented in the early 1950s, uses the magnetic properties of electric pulses *(pages 40-42)* to store data on the polished metal surface of a rapidly rotating cylinder. A series of read/write heads, each corresponding to a data track around the circumference of the drum, records and recovers the data, which passes between computer and drum through an input/output gate. Drums were so slow that they rarely saw duty as computer memory. Instead, they were used as storage devices until supplanted in the 1960s by modern, high-performance hard-disk drives *(pages 60-61)*.

performed flawlessly—but to no great end. Much to Lukoff's disappointment, the EDVAC team turned thumbs down on his invention, choosing instead the well-proven oven method of temperature control.

MEMORY GOES TUBULAR

While Lukoff struggled to perfect the serial delay line, Fred Williams, a researcher at England's Manchester University, had begun crafting another apparatus, also serial in nature, that would give rise to the first random-access computer memory. Built by Williams in 1946, the device exploited the workings of the cathode-ray tube, or CRT, which is best known today as the display screen of televisions and personal computers.

Williams knew that at every point where the electron beam of a CRT struck the phosphor-coated interior of the tube, a charged "dot" was created that would linger there briefly before it faded away. If the beam was moved slightly instead of being kept still, it left a charged "dash." By depositing such dots and dashes on the tube in a series of horizontal sweeps, the electron beam could be used to write, or store, the ones and zeros of binary information. The recording method was serial because the beam wrote the binary digits of a computer word one after another in rows on the cathode-ray tube.

The electron beam functioned as a reading mechanism, too. At low power (in order not to alter the previously recorded information), the beam swept back and forth across the charged spots inside the tube, causing a current to leak through the glass at those points to the front of the tube. The strength of the current differed slightly for a dot or a dash, enough for a metallic screen fitted over the face of the tube to distinguish between ones and zeros and then pass them to a computer's CPU.

There was one difficulty still remaining: The dots and dashes faded from the tube just two-tenths of a second after they appeared. If Williams's new kind of memory was to be of any consequence, he would have to find a way to correct this spontaneous self-erasure. Williams discovered that the writing process left a sprinkling of electrons surrounding each dot and dash on the tube. He devised a system in which the low-power beam constantly scanned the face of a tube on which data had been recorded. Whenever an electron smudge signaled the proximity of a dot or dash, a distinctive current was generated in the metallic screen. Instantly, the power of the beam was boosted to rewrite the information in the same location.

By the end of 1947, Williams and a colleague of his, Tom Kilburn, had produced a prototype Williams tube—at some point the invention had acquired the name of the inventor—that was capable of storing 1,000 bits of information. Only six months later, the two unveiled a similar device boasting a capacity of several thousand bits and access to data, though still serial, ten times faster than that offered by a delay line.

During the spring of 1948, word of the breakthrough that Fred Williams had achieved reached the Institute for Advanced Study in Princeton, New Jersey. There a team of engineers working under the leadership of John von Neumann had reached an impasse in their effort to construct a new general-purpose scientific machine that was to be called the IAS computer. In the course of the preceding two years the von Neumann team had considered a number of

Magnetic Memory for Computers

Core memory takes advantage of the intimate relationship between electricity and magnetism to provide total recall for computers. A current in a wire creates a magnetic field around it. The orientation of the magnetism is determined by the current flow, according to what physicists call the right-hand rule: With the thumb pointed in the direction of the current, the fingers of the right hand curl in the direction of the magnetic field. This field can permanently magnetize a doughnut-shaped core made of ferromagnetic materials. Magnetizing the core in one direction—counterclockwise as shown on this and the following pages—stores a one. Reversing the current magnetizes the core in the other direction, storing a zero.

For a core to be magnetized, the current must exceed the magnetic threshold of the ferromagnetic material in the doughnut. Yet the current need not be supplied by a single wire. Two wires, for example, can each supply half the current. Furthermore, the wires need not be parallel; as long as current flows through the wires in the direction indicated by the right-hand rule, they may even cross at right angles to each other *(below)*. The concept of coincident currents—two currents, each contributing half the field necessary to magnetize a core—makes this type of memory practical *(overleaf)*.

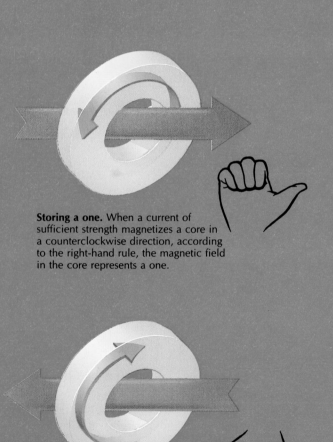

Storing a one. When a current of sufficient strength magnetizes a core in a counterclockwise direction, according to the right-hand rule, the magnetic field in the core represents a one.

Storing a zero. A clockwise field in a core, induced by a current that is flowing in a direction opposite to the one above, stands for a zero.

Splitting the current. Each of the wires threaded through the core above carries half the current needed to magnetize it. Alone, neither current would affect the core, but when the two currents join forces—or coincide— the core is magnetized according to a double application of the right-hand rule, in this case as a one. Reversing the current in both wires flips the magnetic field of the core, marking it as a zero.

Storing Bits and Getting Them Back

The magnetization of cores by means of currents traveling through two wires simultaneously is the basis for turning a scientific curio into a potent computer memory. The simplest version is a two-dimensional grid. It consists of an insulating frame filled in with a weave of horizontal and vertical wires. At each intersection hangs a tiny ring of ferromagnetic material no more than 1/50 inch in diameter.

Any one of the rings in the grid can be selected individually to store a bit—either a one or a zero—simply by energizing the wires that pass through it (below, left). Because the rings can be activated in any sequence imaginable, core memory provides true random access to data.

Recalling the contents of core memory combines the principle of coincident current with the fact that a changing magnetic field generates a current in a nearby wire. By being programmed to note the presence or absence of this current, a computer can discern whether a core contains a one or a zero (below, right).

As a practical matter, the capacity of two-dimensional core memories is limited by their size. A memory that had a capacity of one million bits would require 1,000 vertical wires and 1,000 horizontal wires, each of which would have to have a control circuit within the computer. In order to reduce the number of these circuits, there are smaller two-dimensional panels of core memory lined up one behind the other in a three-dimensional array (right). In this kind of arrangement, sixteen panels of 256 horizontal wires and 256 vertical wires each yield more than one million bits of storage; instead of there being more than 2,000 wires to control, however, there are fewer than 600.

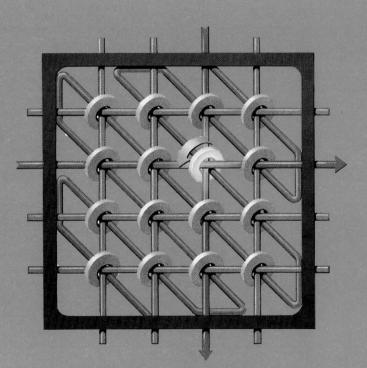

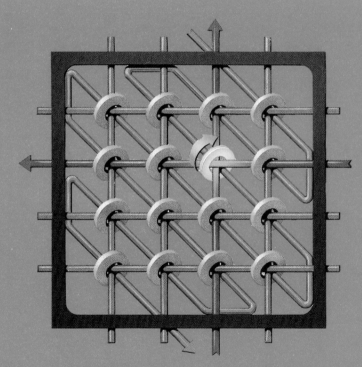

Writing a bit. A panel of core memory consists of horizontal and vertical write wires, threaded through cores, that are used to store—or write—data bits into the memory by magnetizing individual cores. A sense wire (blue), snaking diagonally through the panel, is used for reading the memory (right). To store a bit at a core, the two wires passing through it are energized (red), each with half the current necessary to magnetize the core in accordance with the right-hand rule. The core highlighted in this drawing is being used to store a one.

Reading the bit. To determine whether a core contains a one or a zero, the appropriate wires are energized with the currents necessary to magnetize the doughnut as a zero. Thus, a core storing a one has the magnetization reversed, the one becoming a zero. This event generates a voltage pulse in the sense wire. Detecting the pulse, the computer notes the content of the core as a one, then reverses the currents through the wires to erase the zero and restore the one. When the same technique is used to read a core containing a zero, the magnetization is unchanged, and the computer interprets the absence of a voltage pulse as the opposite of a one.

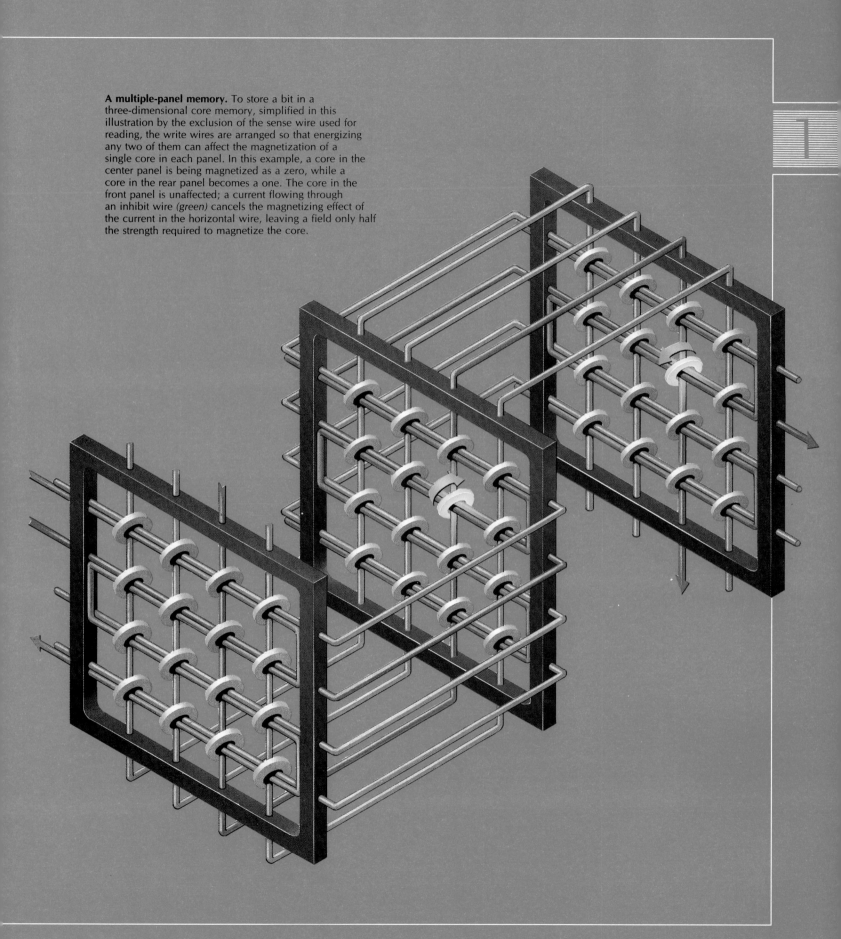

A multiple-panel memory. To store a bit in a three-dimensional core memory, simplified in this illustration by the exclusion of the sense wire used for reading, the write wires are arranged so that energizing any two of them can affect the magnetization of a single core in each panel. In this example, a core in the center panel is being magnetized as a zero, while a core in the rear panel becomes a one. The core in the front panel is unaffected; a current flowing through an inhibit wire (green) cancels the magnetizing effect of the current in the horizontal wire, leaving a field only half the strength required to magnetize the core.

different high-speed memory devices—and rejected them as unreliable.

The most promising candidate left in the running was the Selectron tube, progeny of an inventor at RCA Laboratories named Jan Rajchman. Like Williams's invention, the Selectron tube employed an electron beam in a glass tube. However, its storage elements were not glowing regions of a phosphor coating on glass, but nickel-plated steel eyelets embedded in an insulating wafer of mica. To represent ones and zeros, the eyelets were either charged by the electron beam or not. Mica's natural brittleness complicated the process of embedding the eyelets. This and other manufacturing difficulties made the tubes expensive. Furthermore, a Selectron tube could hold just 256 bits—1/16 the capacity Rajchman had projected.

Thus when IAS engineers read of Fred Williams's success in connecting to a computer a version of his innovation capable of storing thousands of bits, they hastened to try it out. One of the IAS team journeyed to Manchester to inspect the device, while in Princeton another team member cobbled up a Williams-tube memory of his own. It showed such promise that von Neumann's group promptly abandoned the balky Selectron tube. Victims of their own complexity, only 2,000 of the devices were ever built.

The novel design of the IAS machine called for a random-access memory in which every bit in a computer word would be retrieved simultaneously, rather than being collected in sequence as the Williams tube offered them. Von Neumann and his group managed to achieve random access by assembling a phalanx of forty Williams tubes that they built themselves, each tube holding one bit of every forty-bit word in the computer's memory. The feat demanded some exacting digital choreography. Parallel paths and timing circuits had to be devised that would usher all forty bits into the computer's central processor at the same time. The group's efforts were rewarded in mid-1951, when the IAS computer's 1,024-word memory performed satisfactorily during a test of nuclear-equation calculations that required the machine to run twenty-four hours a day for two months.

THE TUBE'S ALTERNATIVE

Although the Williams tube was undeniably a step forward in the quest for efficient memory, it was not long before computer visionaries recognized its limitations. The tube's phosphor coating, for example, tended to contain blank spots so small that they were imperceptible to the naked eye and thus could be detected only by the errors that resulted when the electron beam tried to write data in one of these voids. Furthermore, fluorescent lights in a room and even the spark plugs of passing automobiles generated faint radio signals that could jumble the contents of a Williams tube. One computer engineer labeled Williams-tube memory "one of mankind's most sensitive detectors of electromagnetic environmental disturbances."

Thus it was that in the late 1940s a number of researchers initiated explorations of alternative strategies for furnishing computers with the power of recall. Three men in particular would pursue separate courses—though not entirely independent ones—toward the invention of a radical new form of high-speed memory. Called magnetic core memory, it would ultimately render both delay lines and Williams tubes obsolete.

EMIGRÉ, INVENTOR, ENTREPRENEUR

The first of that trio to patent a core memory was An Wang, a Chinese engineer who had come to the United States in 1945. Within sixteen months of entering Harvard University in September of 1945, Wang had earned a Ph.D. in applied physics. He then began working at the Harvard Computation Laboratory under Howard Aiken, designer of the Mark I programmable calculator. Aiken directed Wang to find a way of recording and reading information magnetically, but without the use of relays. Aiken's own research for the Mark I had confirmed that a computer memory with moving parts would be agonizingly slow.

Capturing data magnetically was easy enough, Wang realized, thanks to a phenomenon that had been discovered during the nineteenth century: An electric current flowing through a wire generates a magnetic field, or flux, that circles the wire according to a law of physics known as the right-hand rule *(page 13)*. When the direction of the current is reversed, so is the orientation of the flux. Certain materials—alloys of iron, for example—that are placed within such a field become magnetized in the direction of the flux and remain so, even in the absence of an electric current. Thus the ones and zeros of binary information can be preserved as magnetic fluxes of opposite direction. Moreover, because the magnetism is permanent, there is no need for refreshing a memory based on these principles.

Wang decided that he would store bits magnetically in small iron cores shaped like doughnuts. The core would be strung onto a wire, aligning it with the flux that emanated from the wire and minimizing the current that would be required to magnetize the doughnut.

Retrieving information from such a memory would be as simple as storing it—up to a point. In order to read the memory, Wang intended to send a pulse of current through the center of the magnetized doughnut. Doing so would have one of two effects on the core's magnetism; either the orientation would be reversed or it would remain unchanged. A reversal would generate a pulse in another wire threaded through the doughnut. A computer would interpret such a pulse as a one. No pulse would signify a zero.

Yet a snag remained. Flux reversal erased a core's information, even as it was released. The very act of reading the memory destroyed its contents.

Wang struggled with this dilemma, known as destructive readout, all through the early months of 1948. Inspiration struck during a stroll across the Harvard campus one afternoon in June. As he was making his way back from lunch to the computation lab, Wang recalled years later, he suddenly came to the realization that "it did not matter whether I destroyed the information while reading it. With the information I gained from reading the magnetic memory, I could simply rewrite the data immediately afterward." Wang's insight would constitute one of core memory's key features: the ability to query the memory of a computer without giving it amnesia.

However, Wang had yet to discover a medium that would be suitable for making a practical core memory; even the most easily magnetized materials required a greater amount of current to alter their flux than was available inside a computer. Sifting through some research literature, Wang spotted a report describing an iron-nickel alloy that seemed almost eager to be magnetized. Not long afterward, the substance became commercially available in a form called

Deltamax. Having acquired a supply of the material, Wang fashioned it into doughnuts; he wired them together in such a way that they functioned as a delay line, each one or zero making its way serially from one core to the next and ultimately back to the computer.

On October 21, 1949, Wang applied for a patent on his "pulse transfer controlling device." Although he did not know it, Wang had beaten two other inventors to the punch.

MR. RAJCHMAN REAPPEARS

One of the men was Jan Rajchman, the RCA researcher whose ill-fated Selectron tube had auditioned for von Neumann's IAS machine at Princeton. Like Wang, Rajchman recognized as soon as he learned of the material that Deltamax was something that could form the basis of a magnetic memory. Unlike Wang's linear string of doughnuts, however, Rajchman's scheme featured a two-dimensional array of cores, one suspended at each intersection of a wire grid. The crisscrossing wires formed the basis of Rajchman's chief contribution to the development of core memory—true random access.

Rajchman was able to achieve random access by supplying half the current necessary to magnetize a core by means of the wire passing horizontally through it and the other half by means of the vertical wire. Energizing a single vertical wire simultaneously with a single horizontal one made it possible for a computer to individually magnetize any core in the array. Rajchman called this approach to storing and retrieving ones and zeros in cores "coincident-current selection"—the two currents had to coincide at a core in order for it to be magnetized. The same technique permitted him to extract the contents stored in any of the cores (page 14).

By late in 1952, Rajchman had constructed a functioning array containing 10,000 cores. Rajchman's success persuaded his employer, RCA, to produce his core memory, but because the company failed to perfect the manufacturing process, its efforts never figured in a working computer memory.

The third person to fashion a computer memory from magnetic cores was a graduate student in engineering at the Massachusetts Institute of Technology. In 1944, at the age of only twenty-six, Jay Forrester had been assigned to lead an engineering team commissioned by the U.S. Navy to build the world's first computer-controlled flight simulator. By 1947 Forrester's group had designed a high-performance electronic machine that could react instantaneously to the pilot's actions, maneuvering the cockpit of the simulator as if it were part of a plane in actual flight.

The computer, ultimately named Whirlwind, was faster than any of its day, but it had an Achilles' heel: The thirty-two devices, similar to Williams tubes, that made up its memory were short-lived—they tended to burn out after only about four weeks. At a cost of $1,000 to replace each tube, the Navy was paying $32,000 a month for memory alone, so a desperate search ensued to find Whirlwind a less costly memory.

Leafing through an issue of *Electrical Engineering* magazine one June evening in 1949, Forrester came across an ad for the same material—Deltamax—that Wang and Rajchman had begun experimenting with. Perhaps, mused Forrester, he could use the alloy to improve on Whirlwind's memory.

The system that he envisioned had certain elements in common with the designs of both Wang and Rajchman. Current-carrying wires threaded through the center of doughnut-shaped cores resembled Wang's approach, on which Forrester had heard him lecture. The fact that every core could be magnetized independently of all the others by means of coincident-current selection resembled Rajchman's invention. But Forrester's version of core memory improved dramatically upon Wang's one-dimensional serial access and upon Rajchman's two-dimensional random access. It proposed that the individual core grids should be stacked in order to provide random access to a three-dimensional matrix.

"For the next two evenings," recalled Forrester, "I went out after dinner and walked the streets in the dark thinking about it." An individual core anywhere in the computer's memory could be magnetized by first selecting the grid where it resided, then energizing the vertical and horizontal wires that crossed at the core's location.

A MEDIUM FOR THE MESSAGE

To test whether Deltamax would work in practice, Forrester fashioned some of the material into doughnut-shaped cores and repeatedly ran an alternating current through them. Although Deltamax passed the test—the cores responded by rapidly magnetizing one way and then the other—Forrester felt that the alloy's softness would make it impractically fragile as a memory medium. Indeed, he found it necessary to encase each of the Deltamax cores of his prototype in plastic to keep them from being damaged.

Hunting for a material that would be sturdier, Forrester happened upon an article that described the fabrication of magnetic devices from ceramic ferrites, a family of mixtures in which a magnetic powder—chiefly ferric oxide—was combined with other metal powders. This combination could be compressed into almost any shape, then put in a kiln and fired, like a piece of pottery, to harden it. Forrester contacted the author of the article, Ernst Albers-Schönberg, a German potter who was working at the time for the General Ceramics Company in New Jersey. Concocting a ferrite mixture that would not crumble during firing and that would have the magnetic properties desired was something of an art, but Schönberg seemed to possess an alchemist's touch. He had only to knead the black material with his fingers for a few moments, Forrester recalled, before pronouncing that it "felt right" to him. Soon he was producing the doughnut shapes that Forrester needed.

Forrester set about testing progressively larger memories. As the work progressed, he went from a single grid that contained a total of four cores in 1949 to a stacked array of seventeen grids, each of which contained 1,024 cores, in the early part of 1952. By August 1953, the memory worked without a hitch. Whirlwind's array of Williams tubes was shut down "with a great sigh of relief," said Forrester, and replaced with his new core memory. Thus outfitted, Whirlwind soared in efficiency. The machine's computing speed doubled, and its data-input rate quadrupled. Maintenance on the memory units plunged from four hours a day to two hours a week.

So far, three men—Jay Forrester, Jan Rajchman, and An Wang—had played trailblazing roles in the development of magnetic core memory, and all three of them had applied for patents. A battle over the patent rights to the invention would soon be joined.

The catalyst for future events would be International Business Machines. In 1952, the company won the contract to build the computers for a new air-defense network called SAGE (Semi-Automatic Ground Environment). The machines, derived from MIT's Whirlwind computer, would be equipped with core memories of Forrester's design. IBM immediately perceived the potential of core memory to replace the Williams tube, with its sensitivity to all manner of external interference. This handicap was embarrassingly reemphasized at the unveiling of IBM's 701 computer in the spring of 1953. The 701, featuring a memory bank of Williams tubes visible through glass doors, performed as expected until a photographer stepped forward to shoot a close-up of the memory. The firing of his flashbulb reordered the pattern of dots and dashes on the screens, reducing the memory to gibberish. Following the episode, all 701 memory units were prudently fitted with darkened glass panels.

By the end of 1953, IBM had undertaken to develop for its own computers a three-dimensional core memory capable of storing 5,000 to 7,000 bits. It was to be a stepping-stone to the 100,000-bit memory that IBM planners deemed essential for future commercial computers. Expanding the memory posed no unscalable technical obstacles, but ferrite-core memory was expensive, and the cost of such capacity threatened to price IBM's computers out of the economy-minded business market. However, developments in the manufacture of ferrite cores soon promised to make them competitive with Williams tubes. Increasingly convinced that a lucrative future lay in store for core memory, IBM set about gobbling up patent rights. The company bargained first with An Wang. Of the three men's patent applications—Wang's, Rajchman's, and Forrester's—Wang's bore the earliest date.

INTRIGUE IN BOSTON

Two years earlier, Wang had offered to sell IBM a license for the patent pending on his invention. He had forsaken Harvard to profit from his invention—if he could—and he was anxious over the finances of his new company, Wang Laboratories. "My capital was $600 in savings," Wang recollected. "I had no orders, no contracts, and no office furniture."

In June of 1951, a tepid reply arrived from IBM. The letter indicated that IBM officials would need to see Wang's patent application, which contained all the details of the invention, before the company would be able to take any further steps. Yet even at this time, before the SAGE contract was awarded, IBM's interest in core memory went far deeper than a casual form letter would suggest, for a small group of its employees had earlier started work on a project exploring the possibilities of magnetic core memory. Unaware of that—and inclined to publicize his discovery—Wang willingly dispatched a copy of his patent application to the company.

IBM continued to drag its heels—and conceal its hand. Unknown to Wang, in July 1954 the company settled on ferrite cores as the memory for its next computers, the 704 and 705. The company's continuing reluctance to license Wang's core memory suggested, wrote the inventor in his autobiography, that IBM had "devoted a good deal of energy to determining which patents would govern the commercial use of magnetic storage, and who would ultimately prevail in those patents that were disputed."

On May 17, 1955, Wang was issued Patent Number 2,708,722, which detailed his invention of core memory in 34 claims, precise legal definitions of the device's composition and function. The following October, IBM offered Wang $500,000 for his invention. Wang rejected the offer; in the wake of the patent award he had set his price at $2.5 million.

As far as Wang was concerned, the patent was his, though the award would not be final for a full year. During that time, others representing themselves as inventors of core memory could petition the patent office to declare an interference between their claims and his own. An interference might delay the awarding of a patent for years. Wang knew of Forrester's and Rajchman's work, but he was confident that none of it had preceded his own. Thus, he would prevail in any dispute.

Then IBM unleashed a thunderbolt: In January of 1956, the company wrote to Wang's lawyer, informing him that IBM had uncovered "a third party's pending application which, it believes, will certainly lead to an interference."

THE SHADOWY MR. VIEHE
That third party turned out to be neither Forrester nor Rajchman, but Frederick W. Viehe, a sidewalk inspector for the city of Los Angeles. Viehe, a compulsive tinkerer in his spare time, had invented a number of devices, including —in 1947—an electronic circuit that was designed to store information in a magnetic core. On May 2, 1956—just two weeks before the interference deadline—Viehe issued a challenge that sixteen of Wang's claims for core memory described his own invention.

What Wang was not aware of was that IBM had hired Viehe as a consultant and had bought his pending patent to boot. Based on disclosures that were made later by Viehe's son, Wang accused the company of having paid $1 million to the elder Viehe for his patent—the rights to which, IBM allegedly knew, might hinder Wang's own attempts to acquire a patent for core memory. When Viehe died in 1960, his savings account contained $625,000. Purportedly sworn to secrecy as a condition of his enrichment, Viehe never did reveal the identity of his benefactor.

"My belief," said Wang, "is that IBM came to the conclusion that buying both our patents might be cheaper than buying one of them should one patent emerge as dominant, and they used each of our patents to induce insecurity in the other camp in order to drive down the price." If so, the strategy worked: Wang sold his patent to IBM for the company's original tender of $500,000. Ultimately, only one of Wang's claims was held to interfere with Viehe's patent.

IBM had yet to reckon with Jay Forrester and Jan Rajchman, whose core-memory patent applications were still pending. As Forrester's notebook entries revealed, his scheme for a three-dimensional core matrix could be traced back to work that he had done in June 1949, yet he had waited nearly two years— until May 11, 1951—to apply for a patent. By then, Rajchman's application had been on file for seven months.

On September 25, 1956, the Patent Office declared an interference between Rajchman's and Forrester's patents. Rajchman had contested Forrester's claims relating to coincident-current selection, asserting that he had been the first person to have incorporated those details in a working core. IBM, wagering that Rajchman's appeal would be upheld, negotiated a cross-licensing deal with RCA, Rajchman's employer, in July of 1957; the agreement gave IBM access to Rajchman's patent—and thereby to Forrester's disputed claims, should they be awarded to Rajchman.

IBM still had no say, however, over the uncontested claims in Forrester's patent application, so it tried to strike a bargain with the New York firm that was handling patent negotiations for M.I.T. employees. When those talks reached a dead end, M.I.T.—which as Forrester's employer held the rights to his patent—opened direct negotiations with IBM. In February 1964, IBM agreed to pay M.I.T. $13 million—$4 million more than had ever been paid to secure a patent—of which Forrester would receive $1.5 million. One month later, the Rajchman-Forrester interference was resolved when RCA acknowledged the validity of all of Forrester's claims.

The lengthy drama had been grueling for all of the players. Forrester succinctly described the experience many years afterward: "It took about seven years to convince people in the industry that magnetic core memory would work," he recalled, "and it took the next seven years to convince them that they had not all thought of it first."

Magnetic core memory enjoyed a long and productive life, at least by computer standards. For several years, core memory was the best available, and its decline began only with the appearance of memory based on the technology of the transistor, which evolved into the tiny chips of almost incomprehensible capacity that equip modern computers of every description (pages 23-33). Though little publicized since the late 1970s, core memory may never be extinct. Thanks to its ability to retain data in the event of a power loss, for example, it became the memory of choice for the computer systems aboard the Gemini and Apollo spacecraft, as well as aboard the space shuttle.

Of RAMs
and ROMs

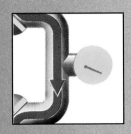

Because computers manipulate information in binary form, any device that has two distinguishable states—large or small, present or absent, for example—could serve as memory for a computer. A simple electric switch is a familiar example of a two-state device. It is either on or off, and the two positions could be used to represent the binary values zero and one.

Early generations of electronic computers used rings of magnetic material to store information encoded as a magnetic field *(pages 13-15)*. Oriented in one direction, the field represented a one. In the opposite direction, it stood for a zero. Silicon semiconductors, materials that under some circumstances allow current to flow and under others act as insulators, have largely supplanted magnetic materials in computer memory. In this technology, each bit is represented electrically. Depending on the type of memory, a one is either the presence of an electric charge or a high voltage; a zero takes the form of a low voltage or the absence of a charge.

The basic unit of semiconductor memory is the cell. Capable of storing a single bit, the cell has steadily shrunk in size until a sliver of silicon little bigger than the flat end of a pencil eraser can now hold millions of bits. Besides making computer memory extraordinarily compact, miniaturization has made memory faster. Transistors, the electronic components that control access to individual memory cells, operate more quickly the smaller they can be made. And placing cells just a few micrometers apart dramatically reduces the distance that data must travel during processing, a significant factor even for information moving through a computer at one-third the speed of light.

The catalog of semiconductor memories includes ROM chips, RAM chips, PROMs, EPROMs, and EEPROMs. Some emphasize compactness and economy over speed. Others focus on lightning-fast operation. Some store data indefinitely, while others serve as temporary scratch pads that lose their contents when the computer is turned off. As explained on the following pages, each type plays an essential role in the functioning of a computer and, though all of them have much in common, each differs from the others in fascinating ways.

Where Bits Are Stored

The bus in a computer, a communications channel between the CPU and the machine's memory and storage devices, is a bottleneck. All instructions and all data to be processed must travel this route at least once. To maximize performance, computer designers try to ensure that data is moved efficiently to the CPU so that the processor never has to wait unnecessarily for the information it needs to do its work.

The most direct route to this goal might be to fill a computer with the fastest memory possible. But doing so would be impractical; even if enough memory could be packed in, the

Disk and tape storage. The slowest elements in the gamut of memory and storage devices, disks and tapes hold data and programs that are not in use. Moving this information into main memory may require only milliseconds, but this is a leisurely pace compared with that of the CPU. Slowness is tolerable if the movements of data and instructions are infrequent and can be done without the full attention of the CPU.

ROM. Read-only memory, with an access time as short as 15 billionths of a second or less, retains its contents when a computer is turned off. This type of memory typically holds startup programs that prepare the machine for use.

Main memory. Data and program instructions brought from disk or tape are stored here for use by the CPU. The processor can retrieve the contents of these dynamic RAM chips in 120 billionths of a second or less, placing this type of memory alongside ROM in speed.

Long-Term Storage

Read-Only Memory

Main Memory

cost would be prohibitive. So computer designers employ a variety of devices to hold data and instructions, the choice of repository depending on how urgently the information might be needed by the CPU. Quick but expensive devices satisfy the CPU's immediate needs; slower but more economical devices retain information for future use.

Outside the computer lie long-term storage devices such as magnetic disks and tapes *(Chapter 2)* and optical disks *(Chapter 4)*, represented below as a tan platter in the map of a computer's memory and storage. Information is imported to the computer's main memory from these devices by way of the bus *(broad yellow arrow)*.

Main memory, the largest area of memory within the computer, is composed of dynamic RAM chips *(pages 30-31)*. RAM stands for random-access memory. As the name suggests, it offers the possibility of calling any word stored in memory to the CPU independently of its multitudinous neighbors. Read-only memory, or ROM *(pages 28-29)*, and static RAM *(pages 32-33)*, both of which also offer random access, are used in limited quantities for special purposes.

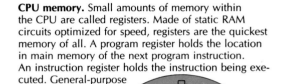

Cache memory. Some computers contain memory made of static RAM chips. Up to ten times faster than main memory, a cache holds operating instructions and data likely to be needed next by the CPU, speeding computer operation.

CPU memory. Small amounts of memory within the CPU are called registers. Made of static RAM circuits optimized for speed, registers are the quickest memory of all. A program register holds the location in main memory of the next program instruction. An instruction register holds the instruction being executed. General-purpose registers briefly store data during processing.

Cache Memory

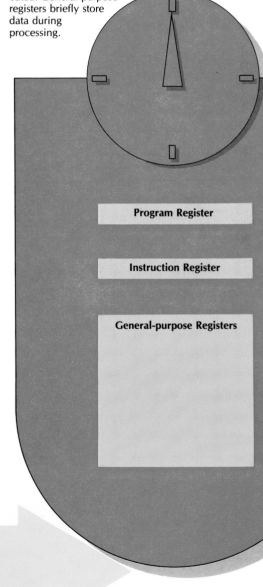

Program Register

Instruction Register

General-purpose Registers

An Address for Each Bit

All forms of semiconductor memory—ROM, dynamic RAM and static RAM, whether employed as a cache or as a register inside the computer's CPU—are alike in one fundamental way: Each stores individual bits of data in multiple rows and columns of cells. CPU registers may consist of just a few hundred cells. A ROM or dynamic RAM chip may contain as few as about 64,000 such cells or more than four million.

Regardless of how many cells there may be—for simplicity, only sixteen are shown in the drawings of chips on these pages—their row-and-column arrangement permits each cell to have a unique designation. Called an address, this designation consists of a row identifier and a column identifier, both expressed as binary numbers. Circuitry on each chip passes the address into its horizontal and vertical components and activates a transistor (box, right) that permits a pulse of

current to flow either into a cell for storing a bit of data or out of a cell when retrieving it (below).

Few computers, however, handle data one bit at a time. Instead, groups of bits, called words, travel together through the computer. Although it would be possible to store a word in the memory cells of a single chip, splitting a word into its component bits and storing each one on a different chip is more convenient. A computer that handles four-bit words would require four chips arranged as shown in the illustration at right. Together, the chips constitute a sixteen-word memory. A computer designed for eight-bit words would require eight chips, and so on. In practice, an extra chip is often added to hold a parity bit (page 86). This error-detection feature ensures that a word is not unintentionally altered en route to or from the CPU.

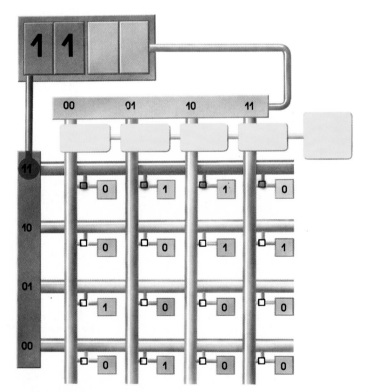

Selecting a row. An address decoder (top) interprets the left half of a memory address as designating the row in which a memory cell resides, in this case the top row. Next, the address decoder signals the row decoder (purple) to send a current through the wire connecting each of the cells in that row. Transistors activated by this current, each represented as a gray box with a red glow, function as gates that open so that each cell in a row is linked to its column wire. Gate transistors in unselected rows remain closed.

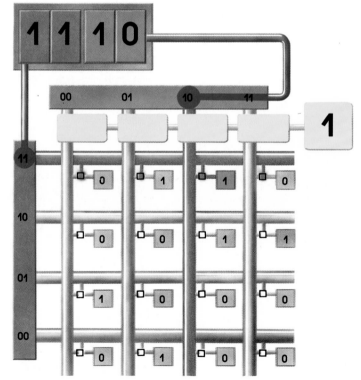

Selecting a column. The right half of a memory address designates the column in which the memory cell resides. Passed to the column decoder, this information completes a circuit through the column wire to a detector at the top of the column (yellow). The presence of this pathway connects one of the cells activated by the row decoder to the detector. Sensing the presence or absence of a current, the detector interprets the cell's content as a one or a zero and passes the bit to the input/output connector on the chip—and ultimately to the CPU.

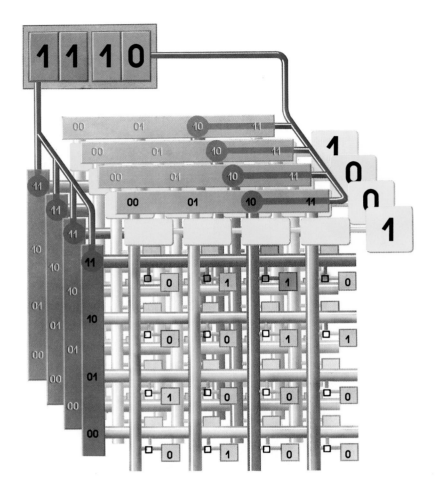

Information by the word. To store or retrieve computer data a word at a time, several chips operate in unison. Each chip's address decoder receives the same cell address, 1110 in this instance. Each row decoder sends a current through the horizontal wire corresponding to the top row of memory cells, as explained on the preceding page. Then the column decoders select the appropriate column wire. Each chip sends the contents of the memory cell thus identified through a detector to the input/output connector. From there, the bits travel together over the bus to the CPU.

Gateway to a Memory Cell

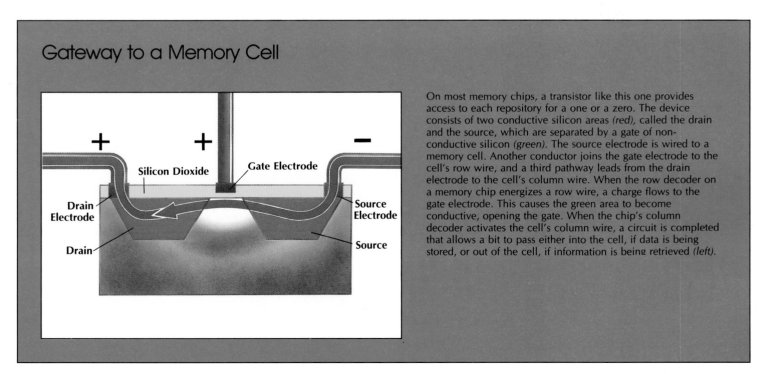

On most memory chips, a transistor like this one provides access to each repository for a one or a zero. The device consists of two conductive silicon areas *(red)*, called the drain and the source, which are separated by a gate of non-conductive silicon *(green)*. The source electrode is wired to a memory cell. Another conductor joins the gate electrode to the cell's row wire, and a third pathway leads from the drain electrode to the cell's column wire. When the row decoder on a memory chip energizes a row wire, a charge flows to the gate electrode. This causes the green area to become conductive, opening the gate. When the chip's column decoder activates the cell's column wire, a circuit is completed that allows a bit to pass either into the cell, if data is being stored, or out of the cell, if information is being retrieved *(left)*.

Circuits for Permanent Storage

Read-only memory comprises four kinds of devices, only one of which, ROM, is truly read-only. In this pure version, the content of each memory cell, a one or a zero, is determined at the time of manufacture. Later, the bit can be retrieved at will *(below)*, but can never be altered. The other three varieties of read-only memory can all be programmed after they leave the factory.

Programmable ROM chips, or PROMs, were first developed to test ROM programming before committing it to mass production. Each memory cell of a factory-fresh PROM chip

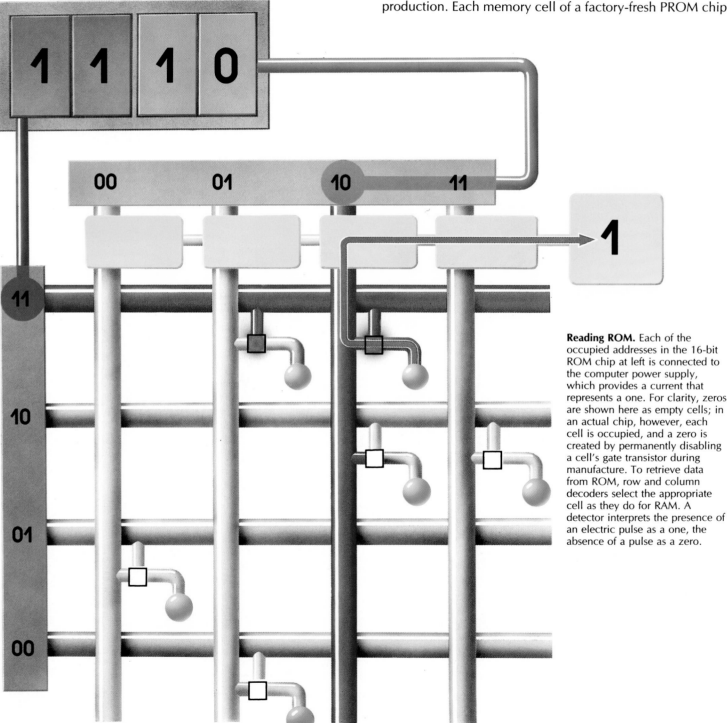

Reading ROM. Each of the occupied addresses in the 16-bit ROM chip at left is connected to the computer power supply, which provides a current that represents a one. For clarity, zeros are shown here as empty cells; in an actual chip, however, each cell is occupied, and a zero is created by permanently disabling a cell's gate transistor during manufacture. To retrieve data from ROM, row and column decoders select the appropriate cell as they do for RAM. A detector interprets the presence of an electric pulse as a one, the absence of a pulse as a zero.

contains a one. In storing software or data on the chip, selected ones are changed to zeros by severing the connections between the cells and their column wires and detectors *(below, left)*.

For PROM chips, this surgery is irreversible; a one that becomes a zero remains so forever. But two other kinds of read-only chips allow data to be erased and rewritten. They are the erasable PROM, or EPROM, and the electrically erasable PROM, or EEPROM. Both of these are built with special transistors that allow the gate between the memory cell and the column wire to be disabled by an electric charge *(below, right)*.

The difference between EPROM and EEPROM lies in the way that data contained in memory cells is erased. EPROMs are restored to their original condition—each cell containing a one—by a bath of ultraviolet light, which dissipates the electric charges that disabled the gates. Some types of EEPROM chips are more versatile. Individual cells can be reprogrammed by reversing the voltage used to create a zero.

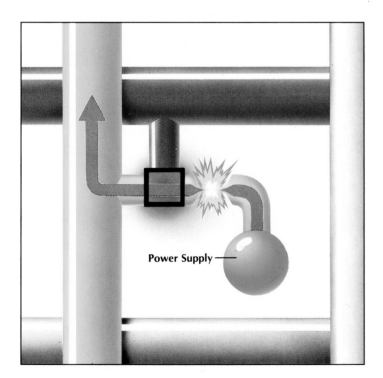

Programmable read-only memory. Each cell of a PROM chip is manufactured to represent a one. The chip is programmed by converting some of the cells from ones to zeros in a two-step process using a special machine called a PROM burner. First, an address is selected by activating a row and column, then a strong current is directed through the cell. The jolt of electricity blows a fuse *(above)*, permanently breaking the circuit over which a pulse could travel from the cell to its detector.

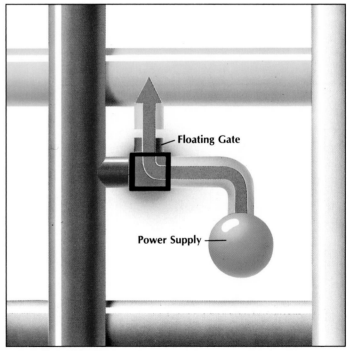

Erasable read-only memory. Ones are converted to zeros in EPROM and EEPROM chips by preventing the current in a row wire from opening a cell's electronic gate. This is accomplished with a transistor having two gates instead of one. To convert the contents of a cell from a one to a zero *(above)*, a high voltage is applied between the transistor's drain and its control gate *(page 27)*. This energy forces electrons across an insulator onto the second gate, called a floating gate *(blue)*. When the high voltage is removed, the electrons are trapped by the insulator. The resulting negative charge counters the flow of current from the row wire, which would otherwise open the gate and allow a pulse to travel over the vertical wire to the detector.

Dynamic RAM Circuits for Main Memory

Dynamic RAM, the chips that constitute the main memory of virtually every computer, stores a bit as the presence or absence of an electric charge in a microscopic capacitor *(below)*, a device consisting of two conductors separated by an insulator and used for storing electrons. A charged capacitor represents a one; a discharged capacitor stands for a zero.

RAM cells differ from ROM cells in several important details of operation. In addition to giving up their contents by reverting to zeros when the computer is turned off, RAM, like magnetic core memory, is burdened with destructive readout

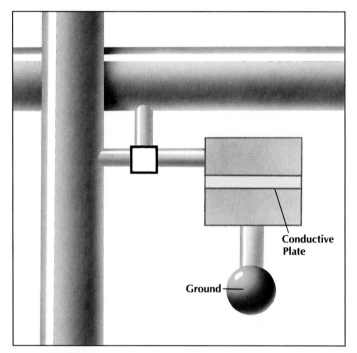

A dynamic RAM memory cell. The capacitor at each address of a dynamic RAM chip consists of two electrically conductive plates separated by an insulator *(yellow)* which inhibits the flow of electricity between them. One plate is connected to ground, an electronics term that signifies zero voltage. The other is wired to a gate transistor *(below)*.

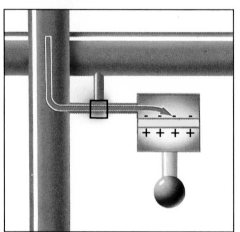

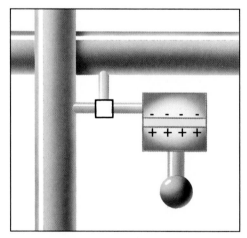

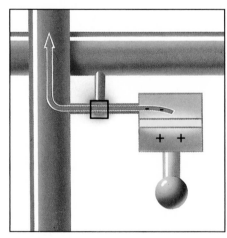

Writing a one. After a memory cell is activated by the chip's row and column decoders, electrons flow through the column wire to the upper plate of the capacitor, giving it a negative charge that represents a one. The electrons attract a positive charge to the top of the lower plate.

Retaining a one. When the current to the row and column lines is withdrawn, the gate transistor is deactivated, trapping electrons in the cell. Attraction toward the positive charge holds the electrons in the capacitor, though they eventually pass through the surrounding silicon to the lower plate and convert the cell's contents to a zero.

Reading a one. When a cell is selected, electrons stored there flow to the column wire, changing the cell's contents to a zero. The pulse of electrons travels to a sense amplifier *(opposite)*, which interprets the signal as a one and sends the bit to the chip's input/output connector. At the same time, the amplifier restores a one to the cell.

(pages 13-15). Quizzing a cell that contains a one extracts the data, converting the cell to a zero; each time such a cell is read, the one must be rewritten.

Furthermore, a capacitor will not hold a charge indefinitely; electrons trapped in a RAM cell escape into the surrounding silicon. To prevent a one from diminishing in charge until it might be mistaken for a zero, the cell is constantly refreshed *(below)*. Hundreds of times each second, circuitry on the chip polls each memory cell. Those containing ones have them refurbished; cells with zeros remain undisturbed.

Because of destructive readout and the ephemeral nature of ones in dynamic RAM, the detector for each column is more elaborate than that required by a ROM chip or any of the PROMs. Called a sense amplifier, it contains circuitry to ascertain whether a pulse it receives should be interpreted as a one or a zero and, because the pulses coming from the cells may be weakened, it has an amplifier to send a strong signal for rewriting or refreshing a cell harboring a one.

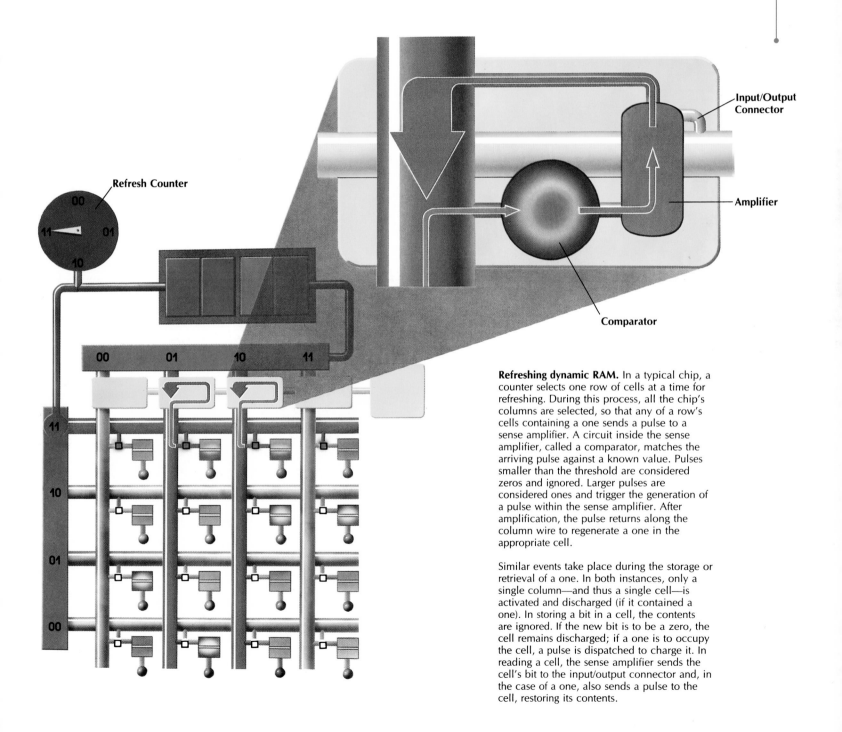

Refreshing dynamic RAM. In a typical chip, a counter selects one row of cells at a time for refreshing. During this process, all the chip's columns are selected, so that any of a row's cells containing a one sends a pulse to a sense amplifier. A circuit inside the sense amplifier, called a comparator, matches the arriving pulse against a known value. Pulses smaller than the threshold are considered zeros and ignored. Larger pulses are considered ones and trigger the generation of a pulse within the sense amplifier. After amplification, the pulse returns along the column wire to regenerate a one in the appropriate cell.

Similar events take place during the storage or retrieval of a one. In both instances, only a single column—and thus a single cell—is activated and discharged (if it contained a one). In storing a bit in a cell, the contents are ignored. If the new bit is to be a zero, the cell remains discharged; if a one is to occupy the cell, a pulse is dispatched to charge it. In reading a cell, the sense amplifier sends the cell's bit to the input/output connector and, in the case of a one, also sends a pulse to the cell, restoring its contents.

Static RAM Circuits for Fast Retrieval

Several factors account for the speed of static RAM over dynamic RAM. Static RAM gate transistors are optimized for speed rather than compactness. No capacitors are employed in static RAM, eliminating the time needed to charge them when storing a one. Refreshing the cell and destructive read-out, with the attendant rewriting of ones, do not apply to static RAM. Static RAM chips are built to handle more power, which expedites the flow of electricity through the circuitry.

A static RAM cell is a pretzel-like circuit called a flip-flop.

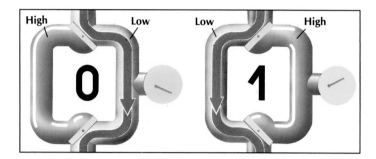

Static RAM as plumbing. Water can flow to the right or left side of the pipe arrangement at left, depending on the settings of two valves *(yellow)*. Flowing water creates a low pressure compared with the pressure where the water is still, isolated by the valves. This pressure differential can be used to represent data in binary form. Low pressure on the right side of the pipes might stand for a zero; high pressure on the right (low pressure on the left) might signify a one.

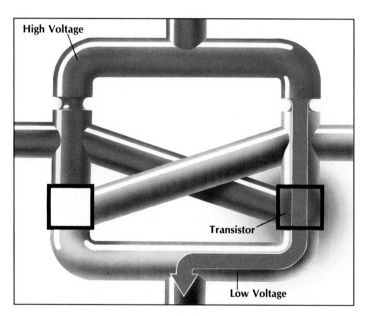

A static RAM zero. Uninterrupted power from the computer enters at the top of this simplified drawing of a static RAM flip-flop circuit and exits at the bottom. Whether a current passes through one side of the circuit or the other depends on which of two gate transistors is activated. When voltage is supplied to the transistor on the right *(above)*, a current flows from the computer power supply to ground, reducing the voltage on the right side of the circuit. Low voltage on that side represents a zero.

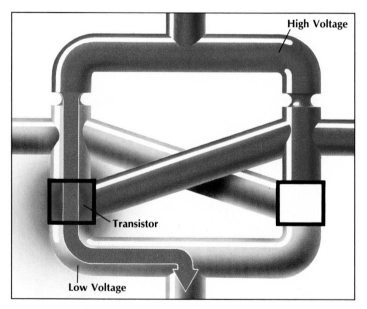

A static RAM one. A one is the mirror image of a zero. In this situation, a high voltage is applied to the gate electrode of the left-hand transistor. A current begins to flow along the left side of the circuit, where the resulting low voltage represents a one.

High voltage applied to one part of the circuit allows it to store a zero. In response to a high voltage applied to another part, the flip-flop circuit stores a one *(below, left)*. An important characteristic of this circuit is that, once established as a repository of a one or a zero, it will remain in that state without further attention from the computer—as long as power to the machine is not interrupted.

Although static RAM cells are addressed by column and row numbers—as are the cells of other types of semiconduc-tor memory—the nature of the flip-flop circuit makes the arrangement of these wires and the functions they perform more complicated. Row wires activate two transistors in each cell rather than one, and the column wire to each cell branch-es, straddling it *(below, right)*.

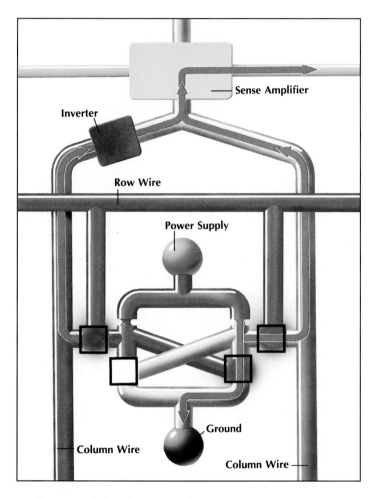

Reading a zero. When the row decoder selects a row of a static RAM chip, voltage in the row wire activates two gate electrodes for each cell, one on each side of the flip-flop circuit. Selecting a column wire elicits two pulses from the cell. A high-voltage pulse transits the column wire's left branch and passes through an inverter *(brown)*, making the signal equal to the low-voltage pulse that travels along the right-hand branch. The detector interprets the pulse as a zero and sends it to the input/output connector.

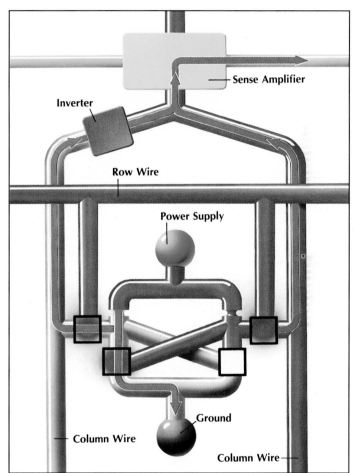

Reading a one. Retrieving a one from a static RAM cell is identical to reading a zero, with a single exception: A low-voltage pulse passes up the left branch of the column wire rather than along the right-hand branch. The inverter increases the signal's voltage to match the high-voltage pulse from the other side of the flip-flop circuit. Sensing a high-voltage pulse, the detector interprets the signal as a one and routes the bit to the input/output connector.

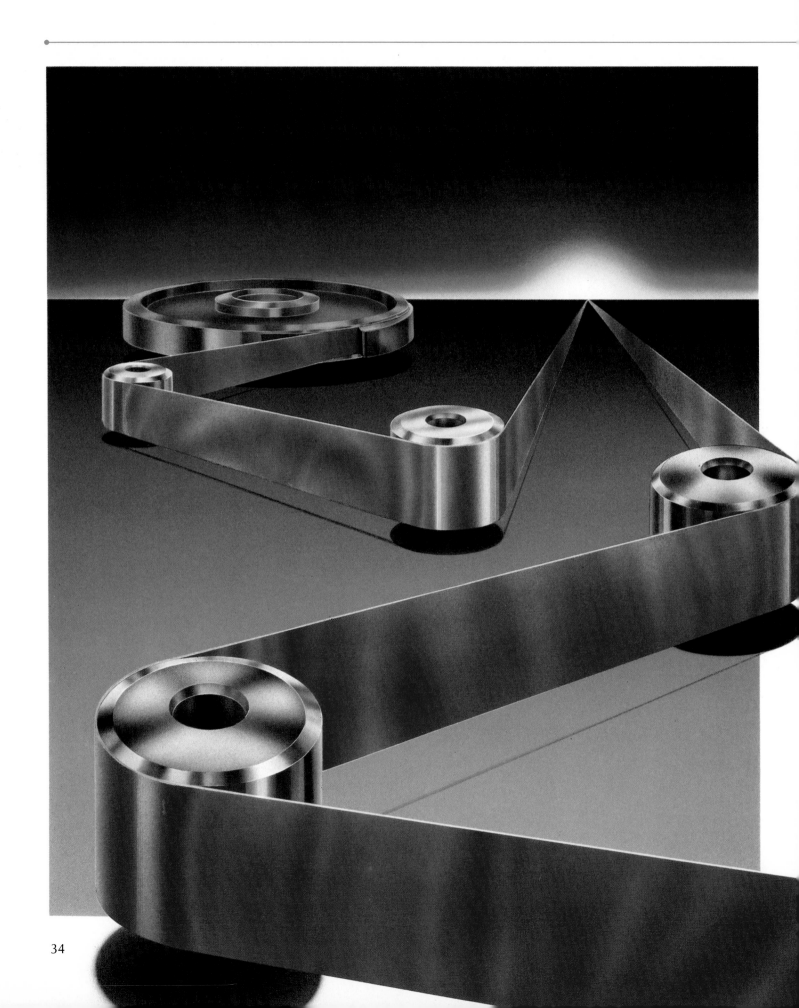

Storage
by Magnetism

In April 1949, a technician setting switches on the Mark I computer at England's Manchester University suddenly deserted his post and ran toward a nearby flight of stairs. When he reached the bottom step, he shouted up, "We are ready to receive track 17 on tube 1!"

The technician's colleagues nearby ignored his behavior. By now, several weeks after the installation of a magnetic-drum storage device in the room above, they had grown accustomed to such outbursts. They knew their co-worker was merely informing the drum's operators that he had readied the computer's memory—a pair of fast but low-capacity Williams tubes—to receive the data stored in track number 17 on the drum. The drum was isolated from the body of the computer because it generated electrical interference that would have garbled the contents of the Williams tubes.

Although the Mark I's designers soon introduced a less strenuous method of data transfer, the machine's two-tiered arrangement symbolized a division of labor between memory and storage that endures to this day. Memory offers rapid access to data but is limited in capacity; storage offers high capacity but exacts a price in access time. Any computer needs both sorts of data repository if it is to realize its full potential.

Over most of the span of modern computing history, the dominant storage methods have been magnetic. The earliest medium was magnetic tape, and it continues to play a major role in the world of computers. Data is stored on magnetic tape by a read/write head, a device that records information by alternating the magnetic direction of metallic particles coating the tape in a smooth film (pages 40-41). To recall the stored information, the head translates the magnetic patterns into electric pulses the computer can process. Compared with other forms of storage, tape.can be agonizingly slow. Access to the stored data is sequential, meaning that hundreds of feet of tape may have to be unwound before a particular piece of information is reached.

Drums were the next type of magnetic storage to be developed. Like tape, they held data on a smooth film—in this case, the surface of a spinning metal cylinder—that was magnetized as it turned beneath energized electromagnetic heads. Unlike the sequential ordering of information on tape, however, the information on the drum was arrayed in readily accessible, parallel tracks so that the heads were not required to search linearly through the entire data store. Although the drum had to rotate before the heads could read the individual data item being sought, the presence of one or more heads per track meant that each item in a track could be found with minimal delay.

A third magnetic storage device, the disk, has come to enjoy the same long life as its tape antecedents. More capacious than a drum but offering the same direct access to data, the thin revolving platter has sprouted two family branches: hard disks, of rigid aluminum, and floppy disks, of flexible polyester plastic.

Whatever form it takes—tape, drum, or disk—magnetic storage makes it possible for computers to collect and disgorge vast quantities of information. That huge capacity has in turn impelled computer scientists to seek ways to channel the data into manageable torrents.

AN ENIGMA

Had not the fortunes of war and a singer's obsession to enhance recording quality produced some vital advances in the technique of recording sound, the art of capturing and releasing computer data might have evolved along entirely different lines. The course that history chose to take can be traced back to 1935, when a pair of German companies pooled their expertise in electronics and chemistry to produce a recording device called the Magnetophon. Its recordable medium was a strip of quarter-inch-wide cellulose acetate film sprinkled with magnetic iron oxide powder. As refined over the next few years, the Magnetophon eventually featured a fourteen-inch reel of plastic tape that could record and play back thirty minutes of high-fidelity sound.

The Germans' wartime use of the device proved a source of bafflement to Allied intelligence workers in England who were monitoring German radio stations. In 1942, the observers began to receive stunningly vivid renditions of German operas, broadcast at all hours of the night, that lacked the customary scratching sound of a stylus in the groove of a phonograph record. Other transmissions from Germany vexed the listening-post operators even more. In addition to high-fidelity music, the radio monitors received live-quality broadcasts of Adolf Hitler's speeches from cities all over Germany. Although the speeches differed in content, they were broadcast in near simultaneity.

The puzzle of the ubiquitous dictator was solved in September 1944, when Allied troops stormed the German-run studios of Radio Luxembourg: Inside they found a Magnetophon broadcasting Hitler's taped speeches. Magnetophons in radio stations across Germany had likewise been used to transmit Hitler's recorded harangues.

Among those enticed by the new contraption was Major John T. Mullin of the U.S. Army Signal Corps, who secured two Magnetophons as war souvenirs in Germany and began demonstrating them upon his return home. Mullin's work soon came to the attention of Alexander M. Poniatoff, founder and chairman of the Ampex Corporation, a manufacturer of specialized parts for the United States Navy's airborne radar scanners. Because the recent expiration of wartime contracts had forced Poniatoff to seek a new line of business for his company, he contacted Mullin, who helped Ampex engineers design their own version of the Magnetophon.

The Mullin-Ampex alliance set the scene for tape's emergence as a recording medium, but tape might never have taken center stage without a boost from singer Bing Crosby. Eager to record his radio shows in advance, Crosby was forever on the lookout for means to improve recording quality. Mullin was invited to tape one of Crosby's shows on his machine, and the result so impressed the singer that he asked Mullin where he could get a tape-recording machine for his own use. Mullin and Ampex answered the request by

delivering a set of Ampex audio recorders to Crosby's studio in April 1948.

In a prescient utterance, an engineer privy to Mullin's demonstration said, "I've got the feeling this development is going to change the lives of millions of people." Indeed, not only did tape's superb reproduction of sound help it dominate the audio-recording industry, but its capacity to hold data would earn it an equally crucial role when another recording device—the computer—came looking for a way to capture information.

COMPUTERS IN A TRACK RACE

Early computer engineers recognized the potential of magnetic tape almost at once. In August of 1949, not long after Ampex presented its tape recorders to Crosby, a company founded by computer pioneers J. Presper Eckert and John W. Mauchly introduced a machine called BINAC (Binary Automatic Computer), whose attached storage device resembled a reel-to-reel tape recorder. The similarities extended beyond appearance: Like the Magnetophon and the Ampex audio recorders before it, BINAC used reels of narrow plastic tape that could store data as magnetic fields induced by electric signals. Because BINAC processed data in five-bit groupings, the data bits were arrayed on the tape in five long rows, or tracks, that ran parallel to the length of the tape. Five bits were recorded simultaneously across the width of the tape to make up a group (technically known as a word); they were retrieved simultaneously and manipulated as a unit by the computer. On the tape, the bits remained intact until erased or replaced.

In September, the Raytheon Manufacturing Company in Massachusetts revealed that it too was designing a computer whose data would reside on magnetic tape, and the race was on. For a number of reasons, BINAC fell behind. Though it ran fine when it left the workshop, the computer never functioned properly for its first buyer, the Northrop Aircraft Company. Meanwhile, its creators had begun work on a more ambitious successor, the Universal Automatic Computer, or UNIVAC. This computer used metallic tape rather than plastic because metal tape was considered more durable. UNIVAC's metal tape boasted eight recording tracks to BINAC's five, enabling it to hold nearly twice as much data. A single reel of tape stored more than one million bytes.

As exemplified by BINAC and UNIVAC, plastic and metal alternated as the material of choice for magnetic tape throughout the early 1950s. Metal was stronger than plastic and less likely to snap, but it weighed more and caused greater wear on the tape's read/write head. Worse still, the razor-sharp edges of metal tape posed a safety hazard.

Despite these drawbacks and dangers, computer engineers in pursuit of greater track density were constantly seeking ways to refine metal tape. One such seeker was Ted Bonn, who had joined the Eckert-Mauchly company in the late 1940s. Bonn's efforts centered on applying magnetic lacquer to a half-inch-wide bronze tape, a chemical process that threw off noxious vapors. "Being an electrical engineer," Bonn recalled, "I would frequently miscalculate the amount of ammonium salts needed and the room would fill with fumes. Then I would throw up the window and stick my head out. But occasionally the door would be opened and the wind would be blowing in the wrong direction; then all of Eckert-Mauchly would fill with ammonia fumes."

Although the first members of the UNIVAC family of computers relied exclusively on metallic tape for storing data, the medium began to disappear in 1957 with the introduction of a stronger plastic tape based on mylar. And when IBM settled on plastic tape for use in its commercial computers, the fate of metal tape was sealed.

HOW TO DRIVE TAPE

In an era when punched cards were the computer industry's preferred method of data storage, a newcomer like magnetic tape was greeted with suspicion. After all, punched cards had holes—visible proof that they held information—whereas recorded tape looked no different from blank tape. To sway doubters, Ted Bonn and his colleagues simply made the recording visible: They applied a solution containing magnetic iron particles to a sample tape, whereupon the particles clung fast to the pattern of recorded bits. When the solvent evaporated, the pattern stood out clearly. "You could pick up the pattern with Scotch tape," recalled Bonn, "then apply the tape to paper and carry it around to demonstrate."

A greater challenge than convincing skeptical customers was to design a mechanism that could spool the tape at high speed and start and stop the reel without breaking the ribbon. As early as the spring of 1949, IBM had begun to experiment with a device called the electrostatic clutch—a balky affair whose operation hinged on the electrostatic attraction between the tape and an energized capstan, or drive wheel. The IBM group investigating the clutch discovered that the capstan's speed varied with the relative humidity of the room in which the mechanism operated. James Weidenhammer, a member of the group, said, "We used to open the pipe on the steam radiator to get some steam into the room and make the thing work." Predictably, enthusiasm for the clutch waned.

IBM eventually developed a successful tape drive, called the pinch roller, that spooled the tape in either direction by holding it clamped between a pulley and a forward-drive or reverse-drive capstan. The pinch roller accelerated the tape from a standstill to 140 inches per second in five milliseconds—and then stopped it just as efficiently. Such high speeds demanded some means of controlling the supply and take-up reels, allowing the tape enough slack to keep it from snapping but not so much that it would become snarled on itself. One day when his colleagues were at lunch, IBM's Weidenhammer chanced on the solution: the vacuum column (page 65).

Weidenhammer's research team had earlier tried using jets of air to blow the slack loops of tape into a rectangular holding tube, but the loops failed to descend any appreciable distance into the tube because the air pressure in each loop caused the tape to stick to the inside of the tube. With the deserted lab affording Weidenhammer the occasion to "think straight," he recalled, "I just switched things around." He inserted the hose of a vacuum cleaner at the tube's far end and sucked the tape down to the bottom; the suction kept the tape from touching the sides of the tube.

The vacuum-column system of tape control, as Weidenhammer's brainstorm became known, was one of the most successful inventions in computer

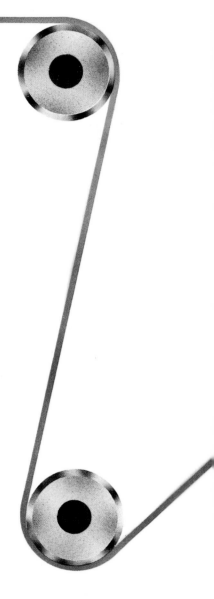

history. Practically every computer manufacturer adapted IBM's design. Indeed, so pervasively was the vacuum column incorporated in tape drives that its sentinel-like cabinet became the symbol of the modern computer in popular films and television.

ENTER MAGNETIC DRUMS

Computer researchers who chafed at the slowness of tape's serial access initially had few options in the choice of an alternative storage medium. The most attractive contender was the rotating magnetic drum, which offered a drastic condensation of tape's expansive surface area through the arrangement of data on the surface of a spinning cylinder. Yet the drum's development was plagued by just as many dead ends and derailments as were its rival devices.

Drums were much cheaper and could hold several times as much data as early computer-memory devices like mercury delay lines and Williams tubes, so they occasionally served as memory devices themselves. Compared with competing memory media, however, the drum's slow speed resulted in snail's-pace processing: Most early magnetic drums featured only one head per track, an arrangement that might require the drum to make a full revolution before it could surrender a piece of information. As a result of this trait, drums figured most prominently as backup storage for a fast memory.

The first working magnetic drum—that of Manchester University's Mark I computer, which demanded such physical and vocal stamina of its operator— gave computer pioneers an inkling of the synergy that would prevail between memory and storage. The drum supplemented the machine's Williams-tube

memory of 128 words with a reserve of 1,024 words, and its location on the floor above the computer itself prompted the Mark I's designers to coin a phrase—"to bring information down from the drum"—that computer veterans still use today to describe fetching data from storage.

In 1952, an electronics manufacturer in Manchester, Ferranti Limited, sold a version of the Mark I to the University of Toronto for nearly $500,000. By that time, the computer's memory could accommodate 256 forty-bit words, held on tap by a magnetic drum with a capacity of 16,384 words. Such a ready arsenal of data equipped the Mark I to perform a wide range of computational tasks, including a portion of the design calculations for the St. Lawrence Seaway. The newly expanded capacity also helped the Ferranti company sell another seven of the half-million-dollar machines, thus making it clear to all that drum storage had come of age.

In the United States, the biggest contribution to magnetic-drum technology came from a handful of ex-Navy codebreakers, who in 1946 had formed a company called Engineering Research Associates, or ERA. Though chronically short of cash, ERA was long on the attributes—vision, innovation, and perseverance—that make for engineering excellence. Just a year after its founding, the Minneapolis-based company began work on a general-purpose computer that would immeasurably refine the operation of the magnetic drum.

The Navy had given ERA a classified assignment: Produce a high-speed digital device capable of performing a battery of sophisticated calculations. The as-

Reading and Writing with Magnetic Atoms

Computing's dominant method of data storage is rooted in the magnetic behavior of a few elements—notably iron, cobalt, chromium, and nickel. Atoms of these elements are natural magnets, and they align themselves into microscopic clumps, called domains, that act like bar magnets. Ordinarily, the domains are arranged helter-skelter, so that their individual magnetic fields cancel one another out. But if an external magnetic force from a current-carrying coil is applied, the

domains line up with the external magnetism, greatly strengthening their net magnetic field. The domains stay aligned when the current goes off, and they reverse direction when the current reverses.

Applying these facts of nature, the read/write head of a computer storage device induces magnetism in the surface material of a tape or disk. (Typically, the material is an alloy of the easily magnetized elements.) The direction of the current from the read/write head determines the direction of the induced magnetism and thus provides the two states needed for recording binary digits using one of a variety of codes (overleaf). Such data is permanent until replaced. It can be read because a change in magnetism from one direction to another generates a pulse in the head.

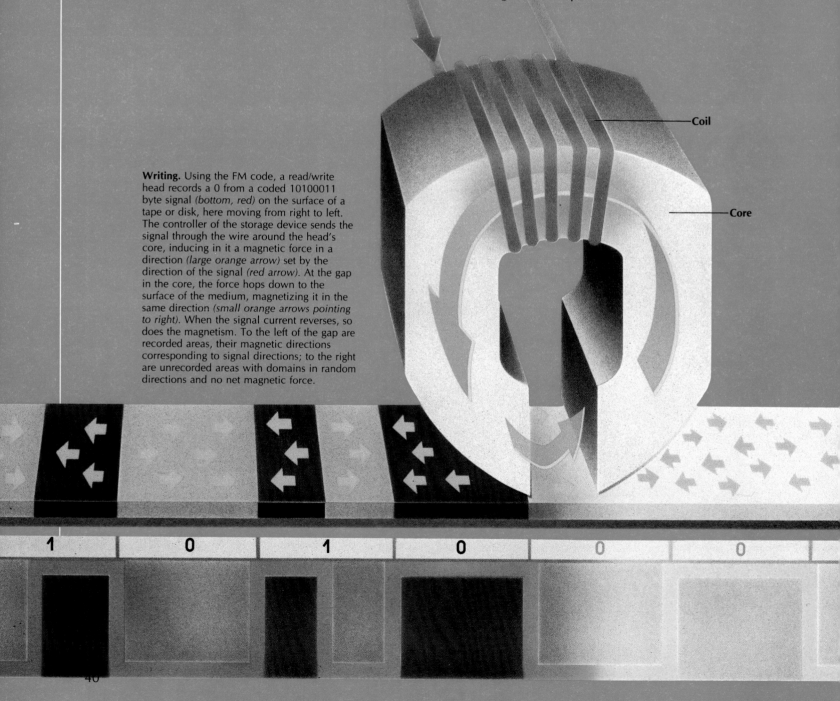

Writing. Using the FM code, a read/write head records a 0 from a coded 10100011 byte signal *(bottom, red)* on the surface of a tape or disk, here moving from right to left. The controller of the storage device sends the signal through the wire around the head's core, inducing in it a magnetic force in a direction *(large orange arrow)* set by the direction of the signal *(red arrow)*. At the gap in the core, the force hops down to the surface of the medium, magnetizing it in the same direction *(small orange arrows pointing to right)*. When the signal current reverses, so does the magnetism. To the left of the gap are recorded areas, their magnetic directions corresponding to signal directions; to the right are unrecorded areas with domains in random directions and no net magnetic force.

Coil

Core

1 0 1 0 0 0

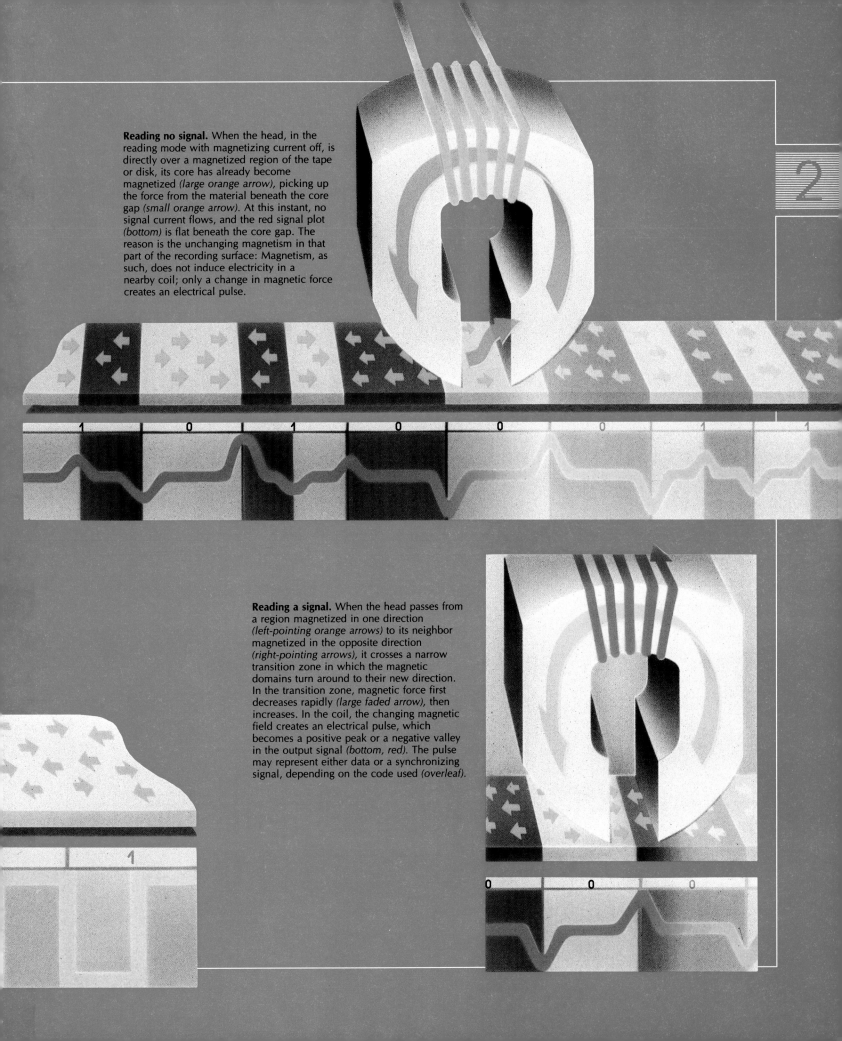

Reading no signal. When the head, in the reading mode with magnetizing current off, is directly over a magnetized region of the tape or disk, its core has already become magnetized *(large orange arrow)*, picking up the force from the material beneath the core gap *(small orange arrow)*. At this instant, no signal current flows, and the red signal plot *(bottom)* is flat beneath the core gap. The reason is the unchanging magnetism in that part of the recording surface: Magnetism, as such, does not induce electricity in a nearby coil; only a change in magnetic force creates an electrical pulse.

Reading a signal. When the head passes from a region magnetized in one direction *(left-pointing orange arrows)* to its neighbor magnetized in the opposite direction *(right-pointing arrows)*, it crosses a narrow transition zone in which the magnetic domains turn around to their new direction. In the transition zone, magnetic force first decreases rapidly *(large faded arrow)*, then increases. In the coil, the changing magnetic field creates an electrical pulse, which becomes a positive peak or a negative valley in the output signal *(bottom, red)*. The pulse may represent either data or a synchronizing signal, depending on the code used *(overleaf)*.

Codes for Accuracy and Efficiency

The magnetized area representing a single data bit on a tape or disk is called a bit cell. In the simplest recording scheme, bit cells are separated by blank spaces, and each is magnetized in a single direction—representing a binary 0 or 1. But such a system is wasteful and error-prone. Not only do the blank spaces reduce recording density, but serious errors may arise if a bit-cell boundary is missed.

As described below, more sophisticated coding systems dispense with blank spaces. They also rely on special rules that reduce the number of magnetic changes and thus increase the efficiency of the storage device.

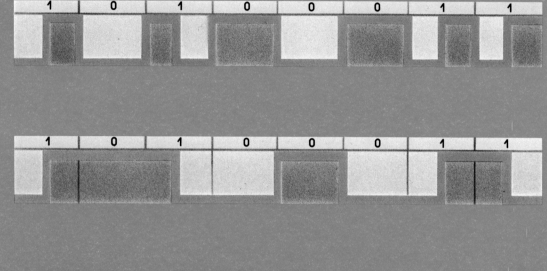

FM. This code (unrelated to the FM of FM radio) reverses magnetism at midcell for binary 1 and causes no change for 0, as indicated in the signal *(red line)* for a 10100011 byte. It also reverses the direction of magnetism at the boundaries of each cell so that the storage device can discriminate between data bits.

MFM. Modified FM encodes 0s and 1s as FM code does: Each 1 is represented by a magnetic reversal at midcell, a 0 by no change. But MFM changes magnetism only when 0 follows 0; then a reversal occurs at the beginning of the next 0 cell. Because MFM requires fewer changes than FM, it is capable of storing twice as much data.

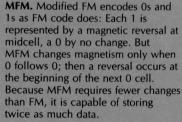

PE. So-called Phase Encoding depends on the direction of magnetic changes. A 1 is encoded by a positive transition *(up in this diagram)*, 0 by a negative *(down)*. Only if identical bits adjoin is there a reversal at the boundary. A lost bit can cause a string of errors because boundary changes will thereafter be misread as data.

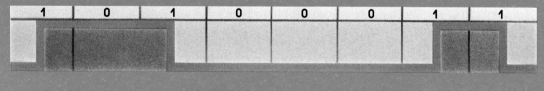

NRZ1. In Non-Return-to-Zero Change-on-One code, a 1 is represented by a midcell flux reversal, a 0 by no change. Although the sample byte requires only four reversals, recording density remains low. As few as three cells in a row without a flux reversal can cause a storage device's controller to miss a bit-cell boundary and misread data.

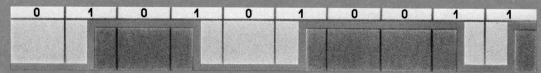

GCR. Group Coded Recording uses NRZ1 rules (a flux reversal on 1) but avoids that code's pitfalls by translating groups of four bits into five-bit blocks that contain no more than two consecutive 0s, that is, cells without a flux reversal. This tactic helps give GCR a recording density considerably greater than NRZ1 has.

signment, code-named "Task 13," was so secret that only the engineers designing the computer were told anything about it. The designers nicknamed the completed machine "Atlas," after the mental giant in a contemporary comic strip. But the computer's exceptional endurance suggested its true namesake might be the burdened Titan of Greek mythology; installed in Washington, D.C., in 1950, Atlas operated nearly twenty-two hours a day.

So successful was Atlas that ERA engineers asked for (and received) the Navy's permission to market a modified version of the machine. In 1951, ERA unveiled its commercial computer as the 1101—binary notation for the decimal number 13. Regrettably, the 1101 was the very opposite of user-friendly. "The most reliable brain in the business," as the *Minneapolis Tribune* described the 1101, came with no programming instructions. As a consequence, only ten of the machines ever saw service.

Despite the fizzled debut of the 1101, ERA's drums—able to store about one million bits each—became the elite of the nascent computer-storage industry. Having blazed the trail in magnetic-drum technology, however, the company proceeded to hand its edge to rival IBM. Even before the 1101 was completed, ERA had agreed to design a drum for IBM's new computer, the 650 Magnetic Drum Calculator. But the deal became a duel when two groups within IBM undertook independent drum designs of their own; upon the 650's release, it became clear that precious few of ERA's design contributions had been included. Worse yet, IBM—in its role as project sponsor—became the beneficiary of all patents resulting from the effort.

TINKERING WITH THE MODEL T
The 650 was the first user-oriented, easily programmable computer. Because it was also the first computer to be produced in quantities higher than a few dozen, it became known as the Model T of the industry. Among its innovations was a self-checking procedure that ordered the machine to stop or alter its routine whenever it detected an error *(pages 85-95)*. But the most significant new feature was the 650's smaller, faster drum. Other magnetic drums of the era spun at 3,400 revolutions per minute, making a complete turn every 17 milliseconds. The 650 drum revolved at 12,500 rpm, requiring only 4.8 milliseconds for a full turn.

The new high-speed magnetic drum—indeed, the 650 itself—might have assumed a different form had not the threat of legal action from an unexpected quarter spurred IBM to alter the drum's design. As late as 1953, IBM's designs for the 650 drum envisioned the use of revolvers—special devices that syncopated the working of two separate heads per track, one for writing information and a second for reading it. The revolvers would have enabled the computer to store one set of instructions or data on the drum even as the machine was retrieving another. In March, however, IBM's lawyers found out that UNIVAC inventors Eckert and Mauchly had been awarded a patent for revolvers just the month before.

Because IBM believed that abandoning revolvers might also mean abandoning magnetic drums, the company immediately launched a search for alternative storage technologies. The most obvious candidate, magnetic-core storage, would have required a costly and time-consuming redesign; IBM likewise rejected a proposal to use capacitor storage, which relied on costly vacuum tubes that could hold just one bit apiece.

While Eckert and Mauchly filed a patent-infringement suit against IBM, a group within the company was struggling to perfect a storage device based on outmoded Williams tubes. The contraption threatened to edge out the 650 drum until IBM's Frank Hamilton managed to find a way to accelerate the drum's speed without using revolvers. Hamilton's drum featured four heads per track; with the heads spaced evenly around the drum, no piece of data was ever more than a quarter turn away.

The revamped 650 enjoyed the sort of success that even the most sanguine of company prognosticators had not dared to hope for. In December 1954, orders for the new drum-based 650 reached 450—nine times more than the company had originally projected. Soon 650s were rolling off the production line at the rate of one per day. By 1962, IBM had manufactured an unprecedented 1,800 of them.

THE DRUM UPSTAGED

While IBM celebrated the success of the 650 and its magnetic drum, a team of engineers in the company's small new research lab in San Jose, California, was quietly refining another storage device—the magnetic disk—that would have an even greater impact on the computer industry. In giving computers near-instantaneous access to immense quantities of data, disk technology transformed the very nature of information processing. No longer would processors have to stand idle while reels of magnetic tape were searched or cards were punched and sorted. The disk popularized the use of computers in areas as diverse as agriculture, health, education, government, finance, insurance, and transportation. By the mid-1950s, stacks of rotating magnetic disks would offer the best compromise—fast access at reasonable cost—of any storage system yet.

The first disks to emerge from IBM's fledgling lab served as storage vehicles for the company's new computer system, the 305 RAMAC (Random Access Method of Accounting and Control). At the heart of the system was a stack of 50 rigid metallic platters, each two feet in diameter, known collectively as a disk file. The disks were permanently mounted on a rotating shaft, or disk drive, and separated from one another by narrow air gaps. Either of two read/write heads could move into the gap between platters to access the disk surfaces, where magnetic data was stored.

To distinguish the storage components from the 305 system at large, the disk file and its drive were labeled the IBM 350. Those familiar with the device, however, preferred to call it a jukebox, a term still used today to designate any similar multiple-disk arrangement.

The idea of encoding data on spinning disks was nothing new. The English inventor Andrew D. Booth had experimented with disks made from paper during the early 1940s, but he abandoned the effort when he discovered that the disks wobbled wildly at high speeds. As Booth and other researchers concluded, disk storage would demand more than just a stable platter; to achieve the desired data density, the read/write head must hover microscopically close to the disk surface. Thus the prospects for storing computer information by disk were dismissed as too remote.

Too remote, that is, until a former high-school science teacher named Reynold B. Johnson proved otherwise. Johnson had been hired by IBM when the company learned he had invented an automated test-grading machine, and in January of 1952 his employers asked him to set up a new research lab in San Jose. IBM hoped to foster innovation by giving its researchers free rein, so Johnson began work with no clear-cut agenda and only the vaguest idea of his mission. "If you take this job, Rey," IBM's engineering director told him, "I should warn you that you're not going to get much guidance from me or anyone else."

SCRUBBING THE TUB

If anyone was cut out for the job, it was Rey Johnson, who proved to be something of an industry sage. "Rey had a knack," said his colleague Jack Harker, "of predicting whether or not the right invention was in the cards."

Within five months of opening the San Jose lab in an abandoned printing plant, Johnson had assigned a team of engineers to a project called Source Recording. The project aimed to automate the transfer of alphanumeric data "from any source"—including, as it turned out, from hard magnetic disks—to punched cards that could be used for computer processing. In so doing, IBM hoped to speed up the handling and keypunching of cards.

Typically, punched cards that contained information about customers or about products were arrayed in long trays known as tub files, and to select a card for processing required that a clerk search manually through the tubs. It was tedious, time-consuming duty, and no one was more aware of the fact than Ed Perkins, an IBM sales representative whose exposure to the nightmare of his clients' tub-file operations had set him on a personal crusade to modernize the process. Perkins haunted the San Jose lab until he had converted Rey Johnson and his staff to his point of view.

Johnson was encouraged in his adoptive quest by inventor Jacob Rabinow, who had written a paper describing a "notched-disk memory array in which each disk was rotated independently." Widely circulated at the San Jose lab, the document apparently introduced Johnson to the idea that magnetically recorded disks could be stacked together on a rotating shaft. Johnson's staff then elaborated the concept into a full-blown scheme for data storage and transfer: Information—generally business records—would be stored in concentric tracks on 50 double-sided disks, and a pair of read/write heads would enjoy direct access to any track on any disk. The heads could read the data to a card punch, allowing the records stored on disk to be converted to punched-card form automatically; or the heads could transfer data from punched cards to any disk in the file for long-term—and high-density—storage.

Johnson was so taken with the plan that in January 1953 he ordered the San Jose lab to begin pursuing disks full time. Researchers less visionary than Johnson regarded his proposed disk file as a mechanical folly. "We all laughed at the first disk array when we saw it in the flesh," noted engineer Jack Harker. "We called it 'the baloney slicer.' "

Johnson pressed on. He asked one engineering team to develop a model for the disk file and another to design a read/write head no more than one-tenth of an inch high so that it could fit between stacked disks. The second team succeeded in "floating" the head at a constant distance from the surface of the disk—

Filing the Data on Tape and Disk

Information stored magnetically—whether on tape *(below)* or disk *(following pages)*—is laid down in tracks that follow the geometry of the recording medium: straight lines on tape and concentric circles on disk.Each involves a different means for recalling the data.

On tape, related bytes are grouped into what is termed a record, then stored together in one or more blocks along the tape. Because the read/write head cannot jump from place to place on the tape, locating a particular piece of data may require scanning hundreds of inches of tape. Consequently, it takes an average of thirty seconds to find a particular record.

Two kinds of tape formats are most common. In the nine-track format, the eight bits of each byte are recorded simultaneously by eight heads across separate tracks in a line perpendicular to the edge of the tape.The remaining track, recorded by another head, holds a ninth bit—the parity bit—used for detecting errors *(pages 86-87)*. The group of bytes and error-detecting bits making up a record is separated from neighboring records by an inter-record gap, which gives the tape drive the time to accelerate to the high speeds needed for reading or writing. The second tape format, serpentine, is mainly used for storing a continuous stream of data, such as backup copies of data on hard disks. Bytes are written one after the other parallel to the tape edge, up one track and down the next. One, two, or four heads read and write in both directions, moving vertically from track to track.

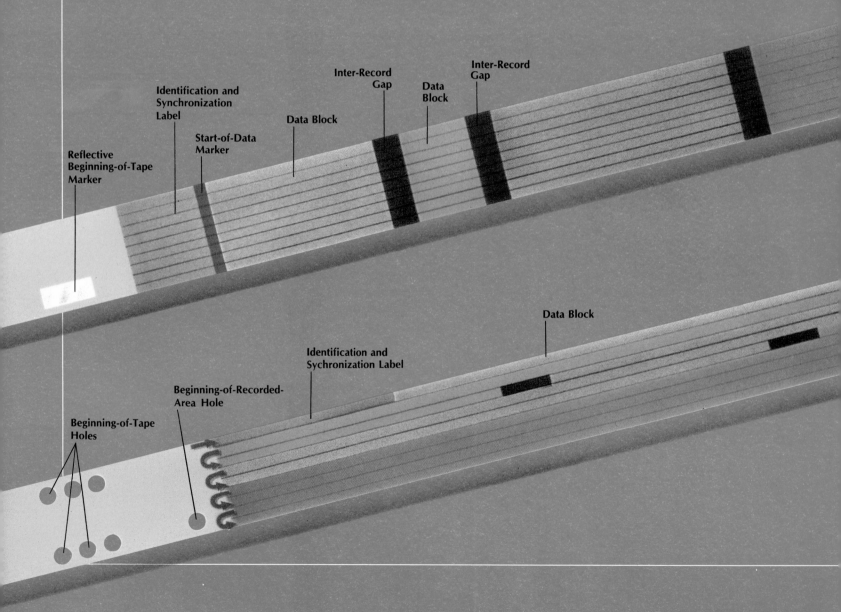

Inter-Record Gap

Data Block

Inter-Record Gap

Data Block

Identification and Synchronization Label

Data Block

Start-of-Data Marker

Reflective Beginning-of-Tape Marker

Data Block

Identification and Sychronization Label

Beginning-of-Recorded-Area Hole

Beginning-of-Tape Holes

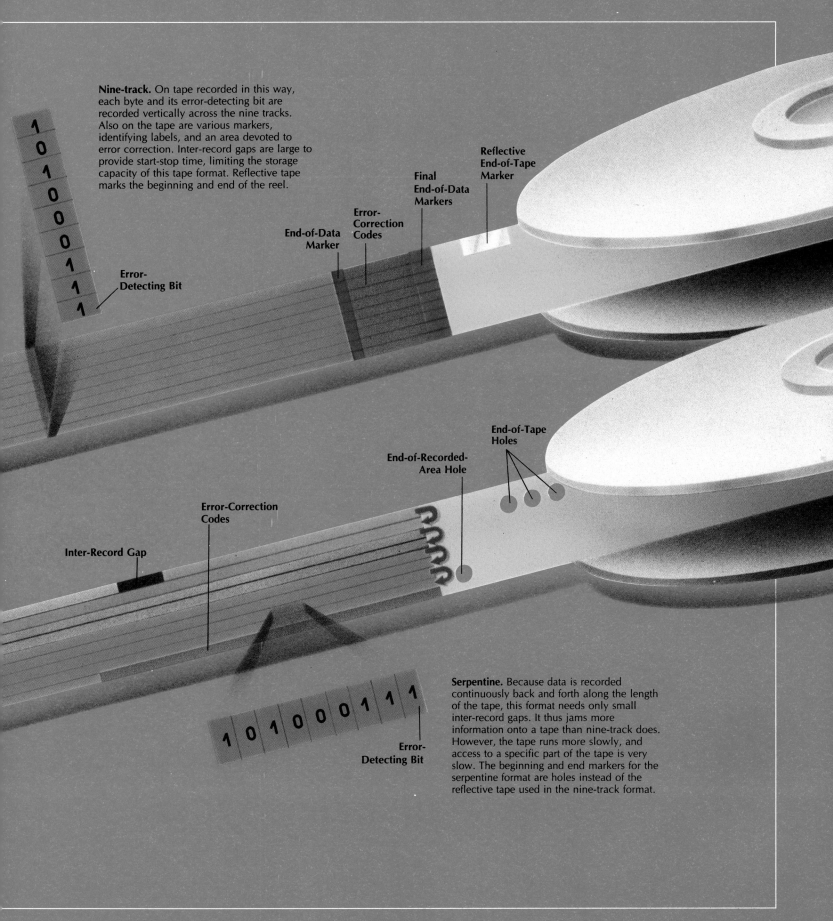

Nine-track. On tape recorded in this way, each byte and its error-detecting bit are recorded vertically across the nine tracks. Also on the tape are various markers, identifying labels, and an area devoted to error correction. Inter-record gaps are large to provide start-stop time, limiting the storage capacity of this tape format. Reflective tape marks the beginning and end of the reel.

Error-Detecting Bit

End-of-Data Marker

Error-Correction Codes

Final End-of-Data Markers

Reflective End-of-Tape Marker

End-of-Tape Holes

End-of-Recorded-Area Hole

Error-Correction Codes

Inter-Record Gap

Error-Detecting Bit

Serpentine. Because data is recorded continuously back and forth along the length of the tape, this format needs only small inter-record gaps. It thus jams more information onto a tape than nine-track does. However, the tape runs more slowly, and access to a specific part of the tape is very slow. The beginning and end markers for the serpentine format are holes instead of the reflective tape used in the nine-track format.

Disks: Circular Tracks for Fast Access

The recording surface of a disk is divided into concentric tracks, which, to aid access, are further subdivided into sectors, like slices of a pie. Data is stored in all the tracks of each sector except the outermost; that one is generally reserved for a directory that lists the names of files stored and a label that identifies the disk and the format used for recording.

Disk systems, unlike tape, do not store records together physically. On tape, each time a change is made to a block of data, such as an insertion in a text file, the entire block is rewritten onto a second tape with the new data incorporated.

When a similar change is made to text stored on disk, the original file usually remains intact. The disk-system controller simply checks the directory for an available sector and writes the insertion there. Thus, parts of a record may be scattered all over the disk.

To locate these scattered parts, the disk includes a listing of addresses on the outermost track. The controller consults this subdirectory and reassembles the file in the correct order before sending it on to the central processing unit.

When a file is deleted from a disk, the sectors involved are labeled as empty in the directory. However, the old data remains unchanged until new data is stored in its place. Thus, accidentally "erased" files still can be retrieved by using a program that bypasses the directory to find the desired data sector by sector.

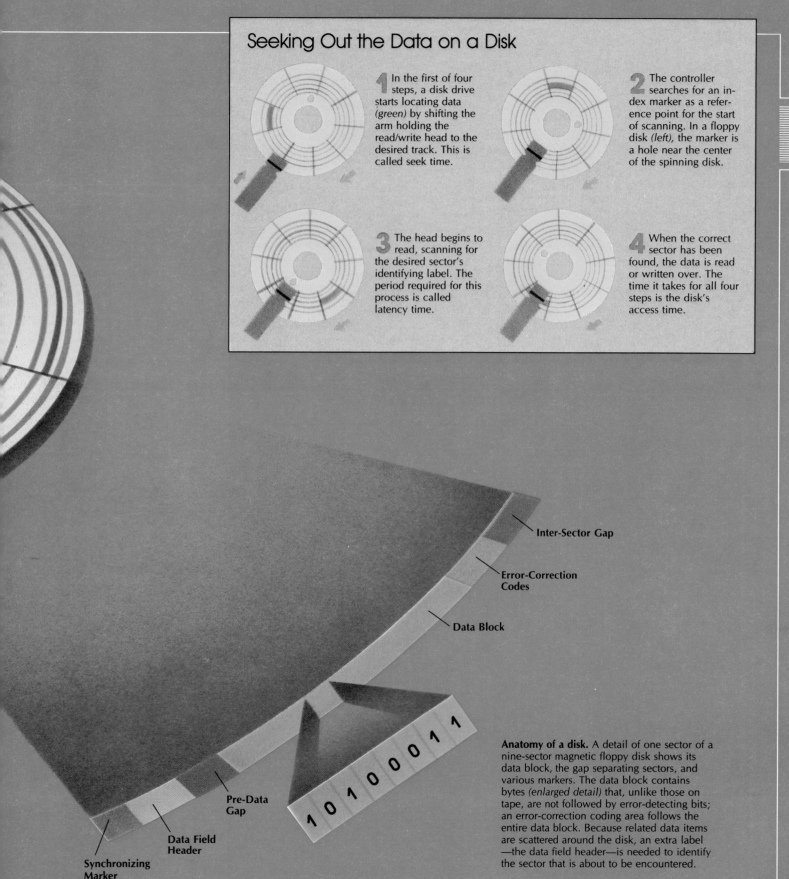

Seeking Out the Data on a Disk

1 In the first of four steps, a disk drive starts locating data *(green)* by shifting the arm holding the read/write head to the desired track. This is called seek time.

2 The controller searches for an index marker as a reference point for the start of scanning. In a floppy disk *(left)*, the marker is a hole near the center of the spinning disk.

3 The head begins to read, scanning for the desired sector's identifying label. The period required for this process is called latency time.

4 When the correct sector has been found, the data is read or written over. The time it takes for all four steps is the disk's access time.

Inter-Sector Gap

Error-Correction Codes

Data Block

Pre-Data Gap

Data Field Header

Synchronizing Marker

1 0 1 0 0 0 1 1

Anatomy of a disk. A detail of one sector of a nine-sector magnetic floppy disk shows its data block, the gap separating sectors, and various markers. The data block contains bytes *(enlarged detail)* that, unlike those on tape, are not followed by error-detecting bits; an error-correction coding area follows the entire data block. Because related data items are scattered around the disk, an extra label —the data field header—is needed to identify the sector that is about to be encountered.

a necessary precaution to avoid destructive wear on components—by means of air lubrication; that is, they pumped a protective cushion of air into the space between the head and the disk.

Finding the right material for the disks was an even greater challenge. Johnson's engineers tested glass, plastic, brass, and magnesium, only to discover that the flattest disks made from these substances wobbled when they were spun at high speeds. Eventually the researchers settled on a disk made from aluminum laminates clamped together and heated in ovens.

Other design obstacles proved more persistent. By the autumn of 1953, for example, the research team had yet to coat a disk with a sufficiently uniform layer of magnetic material. Engineer Jake Hagopian came up with a successful technique, called the spin method, that relied on centrifugal force to cover the surface of a rotating disk with a smooth film of iron oxide suspension. The few remaining roadblocks were dealt with in a home-workshop manner; engineer Bill Crooks added a refinement to Hagopian's process by filtering the iron oxide mixture through nylon hosiery.

In February 1954, a prototype of the IBM 350 transferred a four-line message from disk to punched card and back to disk again. The message read, in part, "THIS HAS BEEN A -AY O- SOLID ACOIEVEMENT BASED ON GWOD WORK." As the errors made clear, the 350 was still far from ready to be demonstrated—much less to revolutionize an industry—but that first data transfer heartened IBM's development team no end. "We were going to make the damned thing work for sure," declared engineer Louis Stevens.

FROM LIMBO TO LIMELIGHT AND BACK

The team's perseverance paid off. By January 1955, the RAMAC disk file was being tested in the field, and four months later IBM announced the company's achievements in disk technology to the press. In June 1956, the first 305 RAMAC computer system was shipped to a customer, prompting an exultant IBM President Thomas J. Watson Jr. to pronounce RAMAC a technological milestone: "This is the greatest new product day in the history of IBM and, I believe, the office-equipment industry."

Despite such billing, RAMAC's disk file would be upstaged by a speedier successor, the IBM 1301, in 1961. Where RAMAC had offered only two read/write heads for its fifty double-sided disks, the six-disk 1301 featured ten—one head for each of the disk surfaces used to store data. That sort of design improvement gave the 1301 four times faster access than the 350. Moreover, a drastic reduction in head-to-disk spacing—the distance at which a read/write head glides above the surface of a disk—yielded such a dramatic increase in data density that the 1301 could store ten times more information than the 350.

RAMAC and the 1301 were merely the first steps in a search by storage designers to increase the packing of data on magnetic disks. In the late 1960s, IBM engineers designed a read/write head that could skim over the disk surface on a cushion of air just 20 millionths of an inch thick, one-twelfth the circumference of a smoke particle (pages 53-69). The head was incorporated in an IBM

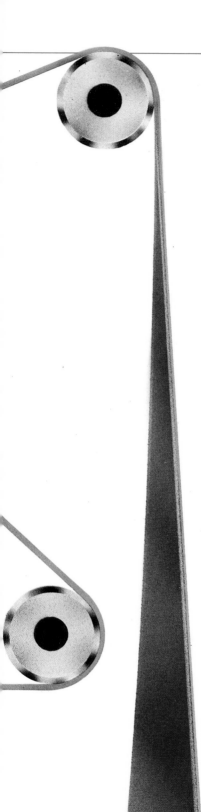

storage device called the 3340 disk unit, whose fourteen-inch disks could store 1.7 million bits per square inch, double the information density of previous IBM disks. Engineer Ken Haughton dubbed the 3340 prototype a "Winchester" because its disk files offered access in 30 milliseconds to 30 megabytes—or 30 million eight-bit computer words—of data storage apiece; those numbers recalled the 30-30 caliber and powder-weight designation of the Winchester rifle that Haughton kept at home. The nickname stuck. Regardless of origin, every hard-disk drive that followed the IBM 3340 was familiarly called a Winchester.

THE FABULOUS FLOPPY

In their first decade of existence, all magnetic disks were made of metal and were thus rigid—hard, in the language of the computer world. Floppy disks emerged only in the early 1970s, around the time when magnetic-core computer memory was losing ground to a newcomer, the semiconductor chip. Smaller, denser, and faster than magnetic cores, chips were nonetheless more volatile; they performed wonderfully until the power was shut off, at which point all the data they held was erased.

Thus, as work proceeded in the late 1960s on IBM's new System/370, a semiconductor-based mainframe computer, the machine displayed a fundamental disadvantage: The memory chips holding the basic operating instructions went blank as soon as the computer was powered down. This required that the operating system be reloaded into memory every time the computer was switched on again.

The solution to this problem, like so many others, would come from IBM's San Jose lab, where disk-drive development was now headed by Alan Shugart. In 1967, Shugart and a team of researchers set out to find a way of permanently embedding a computer's operating instructions in its memory. The group considered—and dismissed as imperfect—all manner of program-load devices: hard disks, magnetic tape, even 45-rpm phonograph records.

David Noble, one of Shugart's senior engineers, then proposed that the operating instructions be stored on a flexible rather than a rigid disk. The resulting "diskette"—so called because its diameter was six inches less than the standard fourteen—would offer high data density because its resilient surface could press directly against the read/write head with no harm to either component.

Made from the same material as magnetic tape, the first disks that the Shugart team produced were so flimsy they required foam-pad stiffeners an eighth of an inch thick. Later, the group's search for a suitable mailing envelope led Noble to the notion that the diskette could spin inside a flexible plastic jacket, or sleeve. A custom-designed, nonwoven fabric lining the inside of the jacket would protect the diskette from undue abrasion and wipe it clean as it turned, while a small rectangular opening would afford the computer's read/write head access to the surface of the disk.

Noble was never properly credited for the insight, yet his protective jacket guaranteed the success of the floppy disk. Here for the first time was a storage medium both handy and portable: The floppy disk enabled computer programs to be passed directly from one user to the next, and in mere seconds a diskette could be popped from its drive and replaced by another containing a different program. Not only that, but the floppy disk was inexpensive and reusable. Such advantages ensured the spread of floppy disks, contributing to a personal-computer explosion that would draw sophisticated computing power out of the laboratory and into the office and home.

A VISIONARY PIED PIPER

Although Shugart's early career had been a study in stability—"I graduated from college on a Sunday and started with IBM on Monday," he remembered, his sense of the potential of portable disks would launch him on an entrepreneurial odyssey. In 1969, after 18 years with IBM, he left the company to spearhead the development of floppy-disk drives at the Memorex Corporation. Shugart took more than 100 IBM engineers with him when he departed, prompting an associate to brand him a "pied piper." Four years later, Shugart—again trailed by a number of the best and the brightest—broke away to form his own firm, Shugart Associates. "I was convinced that the floppy disk was going to be the basic disk interchange for all small computers," he later recalled. Yet in early 1973, with the Apple II still four years distant, hardly anyone had heard of a floppy disk, much less a personal (or micro-) computer.

Shugart envisioned combining a computer processor with a floppy disk and printer to create a self-contained, small-scale business system. Among those reluctant to subscribe to this dream were the new company's financial backers, who insisted that the struggling firm concentrate exclusively on floppies. The rift culminated in Shugart's resignation in 1974. ("If I hadn't quit, I would have been fired," he later acknowledged.) Shortly after his departure, the company introduced the minifloppy disk—a 5¼-inch version of the eight-inch diskette—for personal computers. In the meantime, company founder Shugart had filed for unemployment; he dabbled in commercial fishing for a while, then ran a bar.

Shugart would not reenter the industry until 1979. Personal computers, most of them featuring two floppy-disk drives, were then taking off, and Shugart's former colleague Finis Conner approached him with an idea: Why not offer personal-computer users vastly increased storage capacity by selling a low-cost Winchester, or hard-disk drive, the same size as the 5¼-inch floppy? It was enticement enough for Shugart; by November, he and Conner had formed a company called Seagate Technology.

Five months later, Seagate unveiled its scaled-down Winchester, able to accommodate thirty times more data than a floppy-disk drive, and Alan Shugart was again shaping the future of computer storage. Apple Computer quickly became Seagate's biggest client, but in time the major buyer would be Shugart's original employer, IBM. By the end of Seagate's first year in business, the company had shipped 1,000 hard-disk drives, and within a few years, annual sales of the mini-Winchester would top four million units.

As with every advance in the field of memory and storage, Shugart's disks merely whetted the appetite for more. Computer scientists aiming to satisfy that hunger would soon create a battery of software stratagems that expanded both memory and storage by fusing the two together. The new tactics in turn sparked innovations in the world of computer storage that not even the visionary Shugart could have foreseen.

Vaults for
Digital Data

Ingenuity in the world of computers is perhaps nowhere more evident than in the variety of devices that store data as tiny patches of magnetism *(pages 40-42)*. Some of these devices serve where compactness is more important than capacity; others are huge and manage vast libraries of information. Inexpensive models coexist with examples costing many thousands of dollars. Some are appropriate for applications where a leisurely retrieval of data suffices; others are powerful machines employed where speed is of the essence.

Magnetic storage devices, whatever their purpose or level of sophistication, fall into one of two categories: disk drives, which record data on a spinning platter, and tape drives, which accomplish the same result using tape that differs little from the material used in the music-recording industry.

As a class, disk drives are much quicker, especially at retrieving data. Instead of searching sequentially through information, as a tape drive must do, a disk drive can position its read/write head directly at any point on the disk, much as the tone arm of a record player can be set down at the beginning of any selection on a record.

Consequently, a disk drive is usually the choice where data or programs, overflowing the memory of a computer, need to be stored on-line; that is, where they are quickly accessible. Tape drives, because they are less expensive per bit of data stored, are used for off-line storage of archives and other infrequently needed information where instantaneous access would be a luxury.

A Magnetic-disk Baedeker

Disks for storing computer data magnetically come in two varieties: floppy disks (below), named for the flexible material they are made of, and hard disks (right) constructed from rigid metal platters. Floppy disks are the less-expensive variety. They are cut from huge sheets of polyester, a tough plastic, which have been coated in advance with a layer of magnetic material. All floppies—the original version (disks 8 inches in diameter), minifloppies (5¼ inches in diameter), and microfloppies (3½ inches in diameter)—have a lower recording density than hard disks. However, they are rugged and can be easily removed from one computer's disk drive—

the combination recorder-and-player (page 57) that spins the disk to store and recover computer data from its surface—to that of another.

Some hard disks share the transportability of floppies, but more often they are permanently installed in the disk drive. Removable or fixed, hard disks are substantially more expensive than floppies and are more susceptible to catastrophic damage that can destroy data (pages 62-63). Hard disks are made from polished aluminum platters. After polishing, the disks are coated one at a time with a thin layer of magnetic material, then they are used either singly or in stacks.

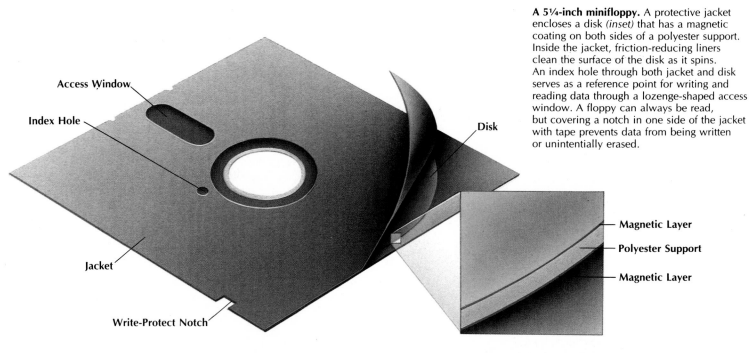

A 5¼-inch minifloppy. A protective jacket encloses a disk (inset) that has a magnetic coating on both sides of a polyester support. Inside the jacket, friction-reducing liners clean the surface of the disk as it spins. An index hole through both jacket and disk serves as a reference point for writing and reading data through a lozenge-shaped access window. A floppy can always be read, but covering a notch in one side of the jacket with tape prevents data from being written or unintentially erased.

Access Window

Index Hole

Disk

Jacket

Write-Protect Notch

Magnetic Layer

Polyester Support

Magnetic Layer

A 3½-inch microfloppy. In this small floppy, a rigid plastic jacket protects the flexible magnetic disk. A spring-loaded door (shown open here) covers the jacket's access window. The door remains tightly closed until the floppy has been put into a disk drive, thus warding off dust and fingerprints. A metal hub, bonded to the underside of the disk, has one hole that serves to center the disk and another hole for spinning it; indexing is by magnetic signal recorded on the disk. Protection against unintentional writing or erasure is achieved by sliding a tab to open a hole in the corner of the disk's plastic jacket.

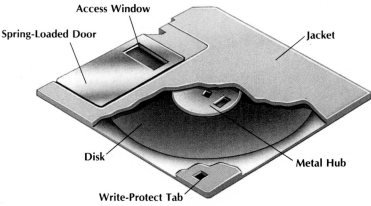

Access Window

Spring-Loaded Door

Jacket

Disk

Metal Hub

Write-Protect Tab

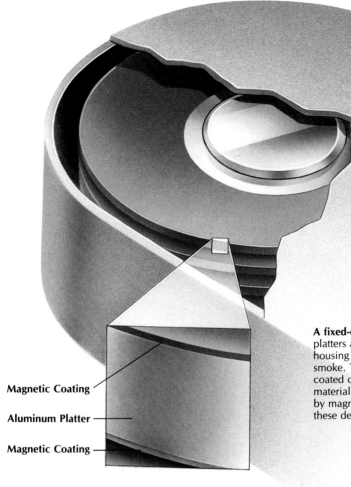

Disk-Drive Housing

Magnetic Coating

Aluminum Platter

Magnetic Coating

A fixed-disk system. In this arrangement, platters are sealed inside the disk-drive housing to keep out dust and even cigarette smoke. The disk *(inset)* is an aluminum platter coated on both sides with a magnetic material. Like the microfloppy, it is indexed by magnetic signposts on the surface. Most of these devices have no write-protect feature.

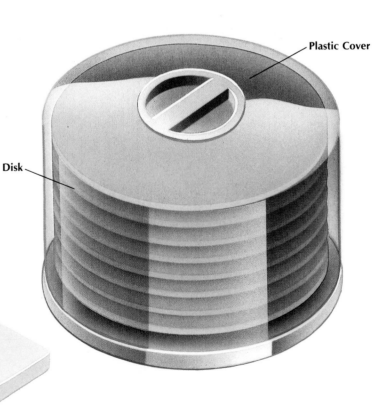

Plastic Cover

Disk

Removable hard disks. Two varieties of disks can be easily extracted from a drive: disk packs *(right)* and disk cartridges *(below)*. A disk pack may contain as many as twelve platters stacked around a hollow core. With the bottom protective plastic cover removed, the stack slips onto a shaft in the disk drive, from which filters bar dust and other pollutants. Cartridges combine the portability of a floppy with the storage capacity of a hard disk. The disk is mounted on a hub inside a rigid shell that slides into the drive; a spring-loaded door and an air filter keep dust at bay.

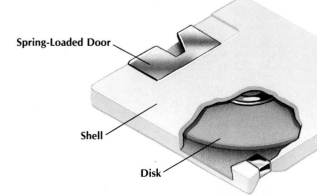

Spring-Loaded Door

Shell

Disk

Floppy-Disk Drives

A disk is nothing without a disk drive, the machinery that spins the disk to record data on its magnetic surfaces and later to retrieve the information. Although the drives for floppy disks of various sizes differ in detail, they have much in common. For example, all have read/write heads, similar in design to the one shown below, that transfer data to and from the disk according to the principles of magnetic recording explained on pages 40 through 42.

To store and recall data, the read/write heads of all floppy-disk drives touch the disk's magnetic material. Despite the presence of liners to clean the disk surface, the rubbing of disk against head can clog the narrow recording gap built into the head. Though this potential source of error can usually be remedied by cleaning, constant abrasion ultimately wears disk and head alike, eventually rendering the floppy unreadable or the drive unserviceable.

Floppy-disk drives employ a specialized type of motor to move an actuator arm that positions read/write heads at the proper track on the disk (pages 48-49). Called a stepper motor, it operates with a cogging, or start-stop, motion. When the motor is activated by a pulse of current from the computer, the shaft rotates a fraction of a degree, moving the heads a calibrated distance. A conventional motor spins the disk for reading and writing in one of two ways. In a bulkier but less expensive system, a belt connects the drive motor to a small turntable that spins the disk. Where space is at a premium, a direct-drive arrangement is employed, in which the turntable for the disk is fastened to the motor's drive shaft.

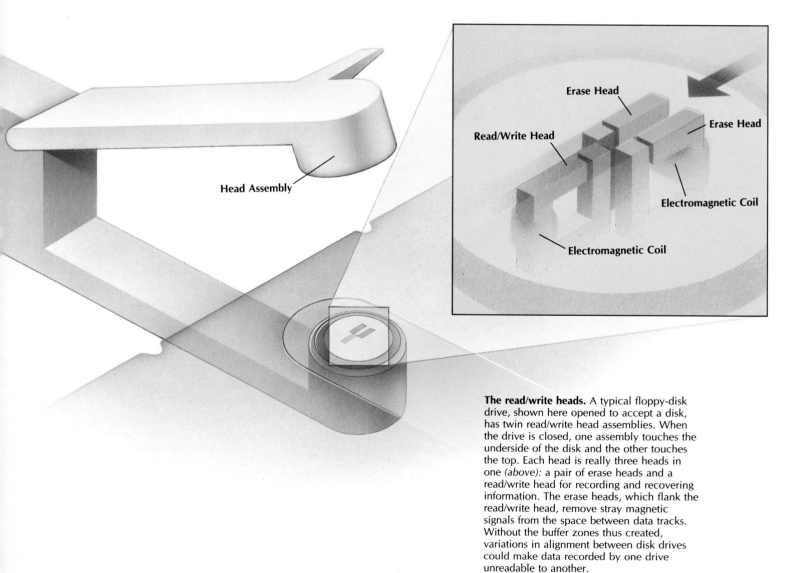

Head Assembly

Erase Head

Read/Write Head

Erase Head

Electromagnetic Coil

Electromagnetic Coil

The read/write heads. A typical floppy-disk drive, shown here opened to accept a disk, has twin read/write head assemblies. When the drive is closed, one assembly touches the underside of the disk and the other touches the top. Each head is really three heads in one (above): a pair of erase heads and a read/write head for recording and recovering information. The erase heads, which flank the read/write head, remove stray magnetic signals from the space between data tracks. Without the buffer zones thus created, variations in alignment between disk drives could make data recorded by one drive unreadable to another.

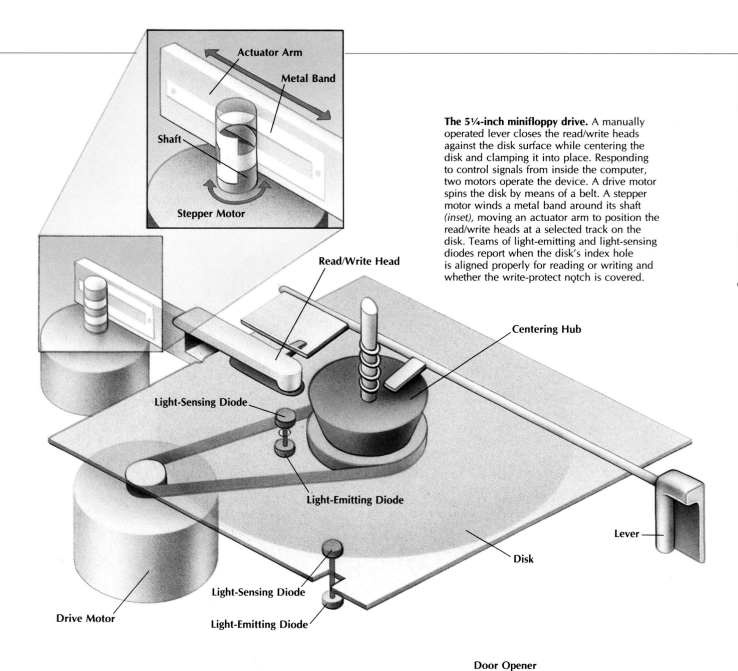

Actuator Arm

Metal Band

Shaft

Stepper Motor

The 5¼-inch minifloppy drive. A manually operated lever closes the read/write heads against the disk surface while centering the disk and clamping it into place. Responding to control signals from inside the computer, two motors operate the device. A drive motor spins the disk by means of a belt. A stepper motor winds a metal band around its shaft *(inset),* moving an actuator arm to position the read/write heads at a selected track on the disk. Teams of light-emitting and light-sensing diodes report when the disk's index hole is aligned properly for reading or writing and whether the write-protect notch is covered.

Read/Write Head

Centering Hub

Light-Sensing Diode

Light-Emitting Diode

Lever

Disk

Light-Sensing Diode

Light-Emitting Diode

Drive Motor

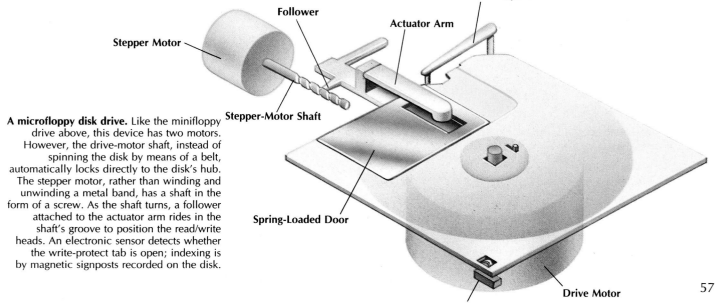

Door Opener

Follower

Actuator Arm

Stepper Motor

Stepper-Motor Shaft

A microfloppy disk drive. Like the minifloppy drive above, this device has two motors. However, the drive-motor shaft, instead of spinning the disk by means of a belt, automatically locks directly to the disk's hub. The stepper motor, rather than winding and unwinding a metal band, has a shaft in the form of a screw. As the shaft turns, a follower attached to the actuator arm rides in the shaft's groove to position the read/write heads. An electronic sensor detects whether the write-protect tab is open; indexing is by magnetic signposts recorded on the disk.

Spring-Loaded Door

Drive Motor

Read/Write Heads that Fly

Simple hard-disk drives, such as the one shown at right, represent the next step in data-storage capacity over floppy disks. Typically, a hard disk the same diameter as a floppy may store between ten and a hundred times as much information. Hard-disk read/write heads do not rub against the platter surface. Instead, they float a few millionths of an inch from the disk's surface on a thin cushion of air produced by the rapidly spinning platter. These flying heads, called sliders, eliminate head wear and disk abrasion, but at a risk. Under certain circumstances *(pages 62-63)*, the heads can crash into the surface of the disk and obliterate any data stored there.

The amount of information that can be packed onto a disk is determined in part by the gap width of the read/write head. A narrower gap magnetizes a smaller area of the disk surface, allowing the data tracks to be recorded much closer together. The gap of a typical slider is about forty millionths of an inch wide. Thin-film read/write gaps *(bottom)*, made by depositing layers of various materials on silicon, are only about half as wide as slider gaps and increase the storage capacity of a hard disk by nearly a third.

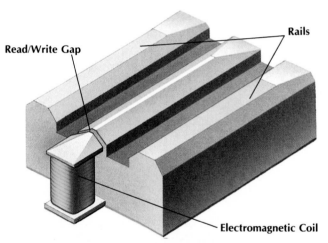

A hard-disk slider. Each platter of a hard disk has two sliders, one for the top surface and one *(right)* for the underside. These sliders consist of three rails that form an aerodynamic unit. As the disk spins at 3,600 revolutions per minute, air passing between the rails exerts a force that balances tension in a spring. Together, these forces keep the read/write gap, which is located near the left end of the center rail, the correct distance from the surface of the disk.

Rails

Read/Write Gap

Electromagnetic Coil

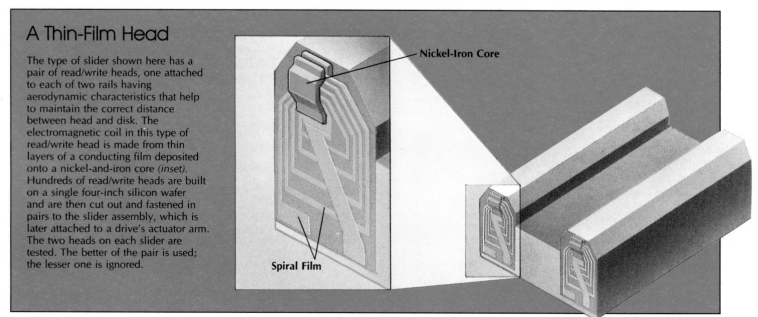

A Thin-Film Head

The type of slider shown here has a pair of read/write heads, one attached to each of two rails having aerodynamic characteristics that help to maintain the correct distance between head and disk. The electromagnetic coil in this type of read/write head is made from thin layers of a conducting film deposited onto a nickel-and-iron core *(inset)*. Hundreds of read/write heads are built on a single four-inch silicon wafer and are then cut out and fastened in pairs to the slider assembly, which is later attached to a drive's actuator arm. The two heads on each slider are tested. The better of the pair is used; the lesser one is ignored.

Nickel-Iron Core

Spiral Film

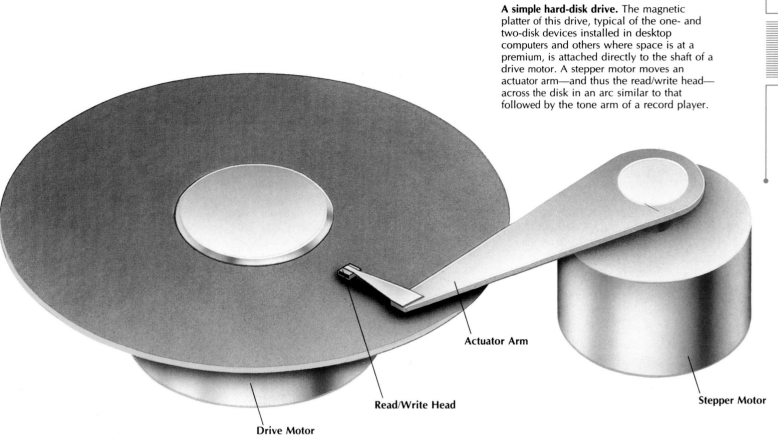

A simple hard-disk drive. The magnetic platter of this drive, typical of the one- and two-disk devices installed in desktop computers and others where space is at a premium, is attached directly to the shaft of a drive motor. A stepper motor moves an actuator arm—and thus the read/write head—across the disk in an arc similar to that followed by the tone arm of a record player.

Actuator Arm

Read/Write Head

Stepper Motor

Drive Motor

Head skew. Rotating actuator arms, though simple and compact, suffer from a problem known as head skew. When the rotary arm is midway between the disk's center and its rim, the read/write head is aligned with the data track. When the head is nearer the center or the rim, however, it crosses the track skewed at an angle, raising the possibility that it will read or write on adjacent tracks. To prevent this problem, data tracks are separated a safe distance and the innermost area of the disk is left unused, thus limiting the amount of data a disk can accommodate.

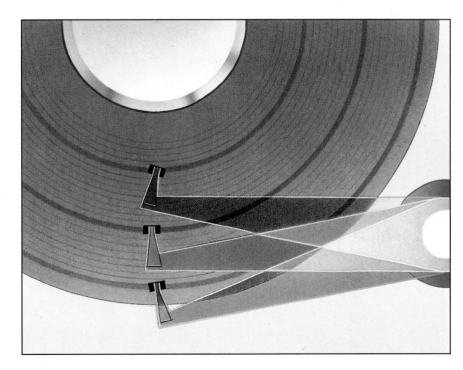

Multiple Disks for Maximum Storage

The most spacious disk drives are multiple-platter devices like the one shown here. Not all the disk surfaces are used to store information. One side of one platter is usually reserved for tracking information *(right, bottom)*. Moreover, in the case of removable disk packs, the outer surfaces of the top and bottom platters usually serve to protect disks in the middle of the stack from physical damage. Even so, with disks stacked up to nine high, such machines can store as much as seven and a half gigabytes of data, almost 200 times the capacity of the simplest two-platter, 5¼-inch hard drives.

In order to achieve storage capacities of this magnitude, data tracks are packed together 2,089 to the inch. This track density is possible because of two factors: the way that read/write heads are moved across the disk surface and the method that is used to position the heads at a particular track.

Standing four feet high or taller, these drives have little need for compactness. So instead of a rotating actuator arm, they employ one that eliminates head skew and keeps the read/write heads perfectly aligned with the data tracks, even those near the rim or the center of the disk. And rather than moving the actuator arm with a stepper motor, which requires wide track spacing, multiplatter drives are commonly equipped with a voice-coil motor—the term comes from the loudspeaker and microphone industry—which allows imperceptibly fine adjustments of head position.

Alignment of read/write heads with data tracks is accomplished with a read-only servo head that uses prerecorded information to adjust the positions of the read/write heads. Some drives dedicate an entire disk to this purpose *(right, bottom)*; others have bursts of such information embedded at regular intervals amid the data tracks. Some large multiple-platter systems combine these approaches to provide the greatest accuracy in positioning the read/write heads—and therefore the greatest track and storage density.

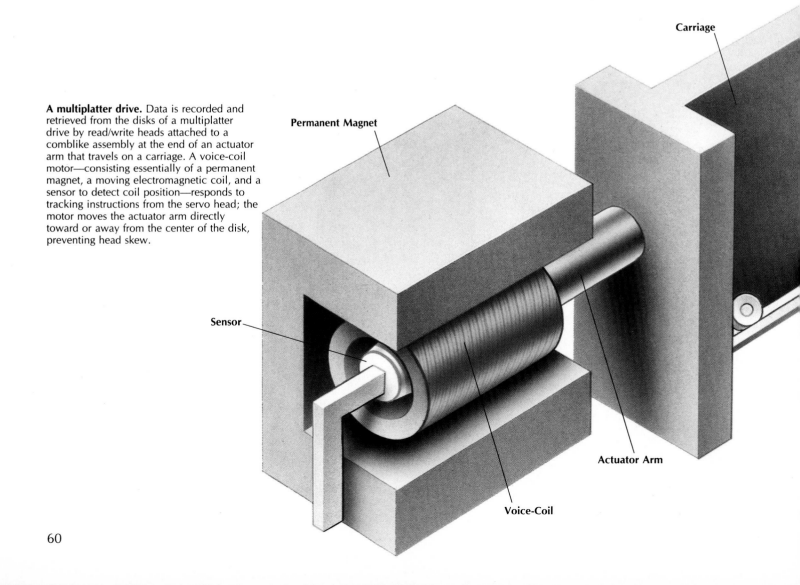

A multiplatter drive. Data is recorded and retrieved from the disks of a multiplatter drive by read/write heads attached to a comblike assembly at the end of an actuator arm that travels on a carriage. A voice-coil motor—consisting essentially of a permanent magnet, a moving electromagnetic coil, and a sensor to detect coil position—responds to tracking instructions from the servo head; the motor moves the actuator arm directly toward or away from the center of the disk, preventing head skew.

Carriage

Permanent Magnet

Sensor

Voice-Coil

Actuator Arm

Servo Head

Homing In on the Right Track

On drives with voice-coil motors, a prerecorded magnetic pattern permits read/write heads to find closely spaced data tracks. On the rapidly spinning disk, areas of opposite magnetization *(blue)*, separated by unmagnetized spaces *(white)*, appear as stripes to a servo head aligned with the drive's read/write heads. The servo head, by moving to where it can read equal portions of adjacent stripes, arrives at the boundary between them *(red line)*, which corresponds to data tracks on the disks below.

Insurmountable Obstacles

A hard-disk slider floating 10 microinches (millionths of an inch) above a platter spinning at 3,600 revolutions per minute has been likened to a Boeing 747 airliner flying six inches off the ground: The slightest obstruction could cause a crash. In the case of the slider, an obstacle as small as a smoke particle can interrupt the disk's operation. It is for this reason that the devices are hermetically sealed and equipped with air-filtration systems to keep them clean inside.

For all the precautions taken, a disk drive can become contaminated. When that happens and the slider encounters even a microscopic particle, inconvenience or disaster often follows. The least of the possible consequences is called a soft error: Data is garbled during an attempt to read or write on the sector of the disk where the obstacle lies. Usually, the next attempt to store or retrieve information at that point on the disk surface will succeed, because the offending particle has been swept aside.

Should the particle scratch the disk, the result is called a hard error; any data stored where the scratch occurs is lost. The most serious damage results from a head crash, in which debris, either by striking the slider or by disrupting the supporting air flow, causes the head assembly to collide with the disk surface and scrape off a part of the magnetic coating. In the aftermath of a head crash, both the disk and the head have to be replaced.

A hybrid approach to disk-drive design incorporates features of both hard and floppy disks and turns potential head crashes into soft errors. This type of device has a read/write head that, instead of floating near the surface of the disk on a cushion of air, is mounted securely to the drive's chassis just beneath a flexible disk that adroitly moves out of harm's way when danger approaches (*opposite, bottom*).

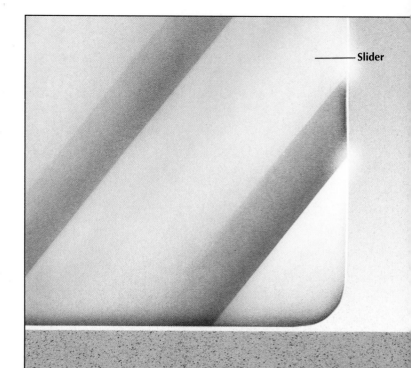

Slider

Microscopic hazards. Shown here about 250,000 times actual size, a smoke particle, a fingerprint, and a human hair resting on the platter of a hard-disk drive speed toward an unpleasant encounter with the slider, floating 10 microinches above the disk surface. With luck, damage from any of these obstacles will be no more severe than a hard error, but any of them could cause a head crash.

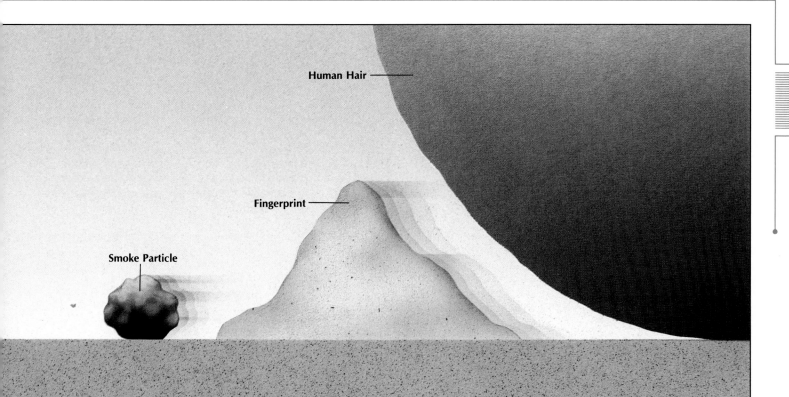

Human Hair

Fingerprint

Smoke Particle

A Disk Drive for Averting Head Crashes

Devices that combine features of both hard-disk and floppy-disk drives instead of positioning a slider near the disk surface, use air pressure to bring the disk close to the head. The sequence at right shows what happens when a dust particle in this type of drive encounters the read/write head. As the disk spins below the head (**1**), air pressure is reduced, drawing the flexible disk close to the head's surface for reading and writing. When the particle approaches the head (**2**), it causes an inrush of air. Pressure increases, permitting the disk to flex away from the head (**3**), and the dust particle to pass. A soft error occurs, but neither disk nor head is damaged. Once the dust particle passes the head (**4**), air currents flush it from the system and normal operation resumes.

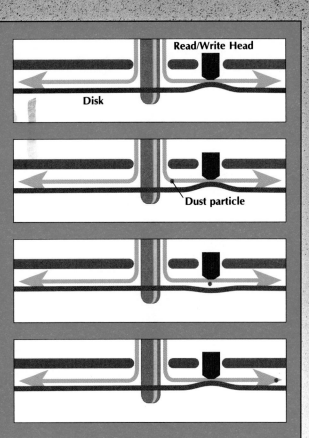

Read/Write Head

Disk

Dust particle

The Tape Alternative

Before the invention of the disk drive, the most widely used medium for storing computer data was magnetic tape. This venerable technology—the vacuum-column tape drive shown opposite first appeared in the mid-1950s—remains popular. Less costly per byte of storage than disks, magnetic tape is hard to beat for sheer storage capacity. A typical reel of tape can store up to 180 megabytes of information recorded on nine tracks *(pages 46-47)*.

However, the suitability of magnetic tape is narrowed by the time required to find data after it has been stored. Searching a long tape for a particular file, even though it is all stored together, typically takes much longer than finding the same file scattered about the surface of a disk. Thousands of feet of tape may have to pass the read/write head before the de-

sired information comes along. A vacuum-column tape drive, which zips tape past the read/write head at speeds in excess of 50 miles per hour, requires nearly a second to find the first file recorded on the tape and may take up to 30 seconds to reach the file stored at the end. Access times like these are no match for the darting heads of a hard-disk drive, which are able to locate a file stored anywhere on the disk in just 30 milliseconds.

Because of this limitation, reel-to-reel tape is used mainly for applications in which the speed of data storage or retrieval is of relatively little importance—archiving infrequently needed information, for example, or making backup copies of data as insurance against loss from a head crash or some other accident.

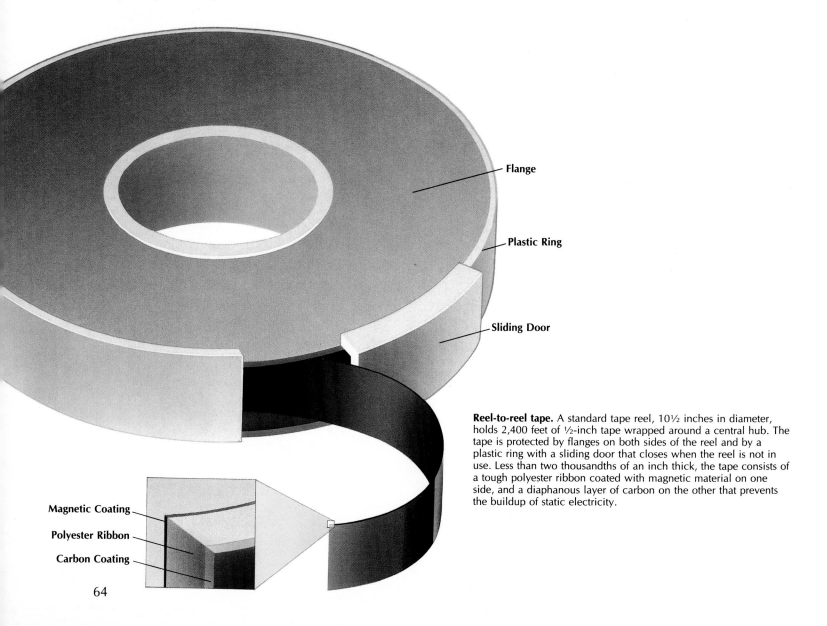

Flange

Plastic Ring

Sliding Door

Magnetic Coating

Polyester Ribbon

Carbon Coating

Reel-to-reel tape. A standard tape reel, 10½ inches in diameter, holds 2,400 feet of ½-inch tape wrapped around a central hub. The tape is protected by flanges on both sides of the reel and by a plastic ring with a sliding door that closes when the reel is not in use. Less than two thousandths of an inch thick, the tape consists of a tough polyester ribbon coated with magnetic material on one side, and a diaphanous layer of carbon on the other that prevents the buildup of static electricity.

64

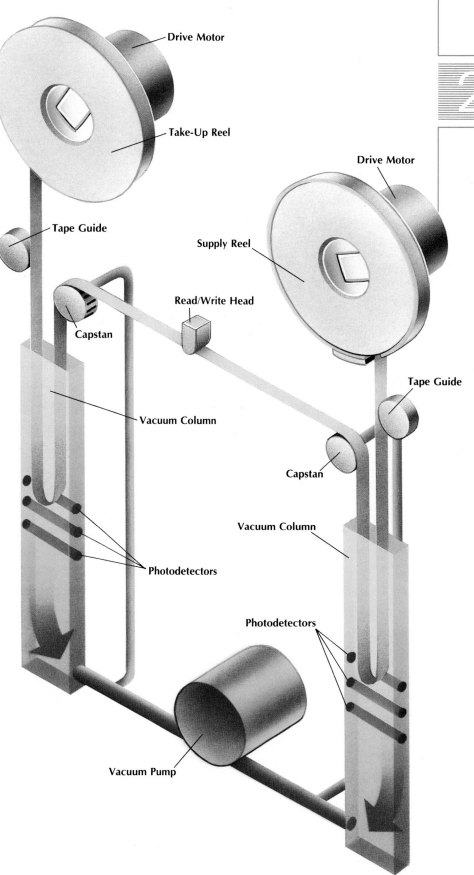

Drive Motor

Take-Up Reel

Drive Motor

Tape Guide

Supply Reel

Read/Write Head

Capstan

Vacuum Column

Tape Guide

Capstan

Vacuum Column

Photodetectors

Photodetectors

Vacuum Pump

The vacuum-column tape drive. This device facilitates data storage and retrieval by allowing the tape to travel at high speed without risk of stretching or breaking. The heart of the system is a vacuum pump. It sucks air through slots in two rotating capstans to hold the tape against them, allowing the tape to be moved past the read/write head. The pump also lowers air pressure in the vacuum columns, drawing tape inside, where photodetectors measure the amount of slack. This information guides the drive motors in spinning the supply and take-up reels so that the amount of slack in the two columns remains nearly equal and the tape never becomes taut.

A nine-track head. The read/write head of a vacuum-column tape drive is actually nine heads laid next to each other (below). These heads, being stationary, can be larger and heavier than the read/write heads found in disk drives. Consequently, each tape head has two gaps—one of them optimized for writing, the other for reading. The device shown here, intended for parallel recording of data (pages 46-47), has a single erase head that clears all nine tracks simultaneously; heads that are designed for serpentine recording have an erase head for each track.

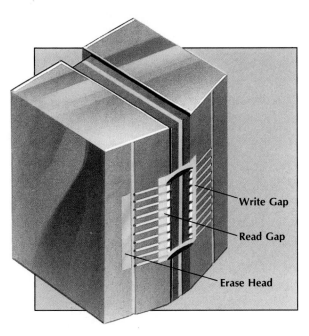

Write Gap

Read Gap

Erase Head

The Convenience of Tape Cartridges

An alternative to bulky reels of computer tape and the expensive vacuum-column drives that go with them is the tape cartridge. Because cartridge-tape drives are smaller and simpler than reel-to-reel models, they are much less expensive. Two types of cartridge, one containing quarter-inch-wide tape, the other filled with half-inch-wide tape, are in common use.

A cartridge for quarter-inch tape *(below)* is self-contained, enclosing the supply spool as well as the take-up spool within the shell. Quarter-inch tape cartridges vary in size. The largest, which hold 600 feet of tape in a package four and a half inches wide by six inches long, may store several hundred megabytes of data, often recorded serpentine fashion *(pages 46-47)* in 24 to 32 tracks, depending on the drive.

The half-inch cartridge *(opposite)* differs from its cousin not only in the width of the tape but in many other details. For example, the shell contains only the supply reel. The take-up spool is built into the drive along with an automatic tape-threading mechanism *(opposite, bottom)*. In addition, some versions of this system record data in 18 tracks, storing two bytes of data side by side. A half-inch cartridge can store 200 or more megabytes of information on less than 600 feet of tape, which can fit onto the cartridge's four-inch spool because the tape is less than half as thick as that supplied for reel-to-reel drives.

Although quarter-inch and half-inch cartridges remain common, they face increasing competition from a variety of tape cartridges originally intended for other uses. For instance, digital-audio-tape (DAT) cartridges, designed to record sound, can be made to store 1.3 gigabytes of data apiece; video tape has been successfully adapted to data storage as well.

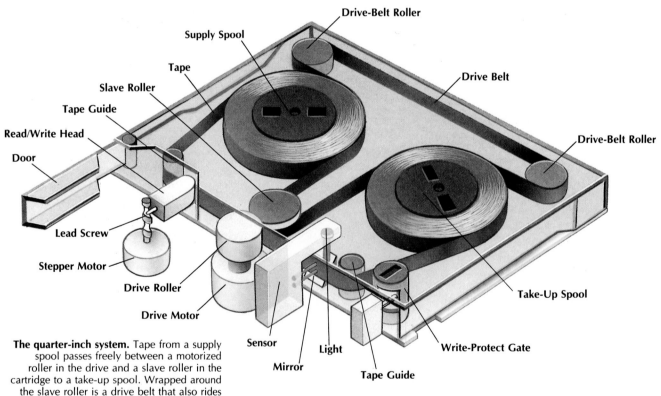

Drive-Belt Roller

Supply Spool

Tape

Slave Roller

Drive Belt

Tape Guide

Read/Write Head

Door

Drive-Belt Roller

Lead Screw

Stepper Motor

Drive Roller

Drive Motor

Take-Up Spool

Sensor

Light

Write-Protect Gate

Mirror

Tape Guide

The quarter-inch system. Tape from a supply spool passes freely between a motorized roller in the drive and a slave roller in the cartridge to a take-up spool. Wrapped around the slave roller is a drive belt that also rides against the tape wound onto both spools. As the belt moves in response to the two rollers, it moves the tape, causing the spools to turn. A read/write head, protruding through a door that opened as the cartridge was inserted in the drive, is positioned at the appropriate track by a stepper motor with a threaded shaft. A system composed of a light, mirror, and sensor detects holes that mark the beginning and end of the tape.

The half-inch system. Tape from this type of cartridge is threaded past the drive's read/write head and onto a take-up spool by a jointed arm that latches to a hook attached to the beginning of the tape *(below)*. Driven by a variable-speed motor, the take-up spool winds tape past the read/write head at a constant speed, slowing the spool as tape accumulates to compensate for the tendency of the spool's increasing diameter to make the tape run progressively faster. After the tape is rewound onto the supply spool, the hook serves to cover the cartridge opening and protect the contents from dirt.

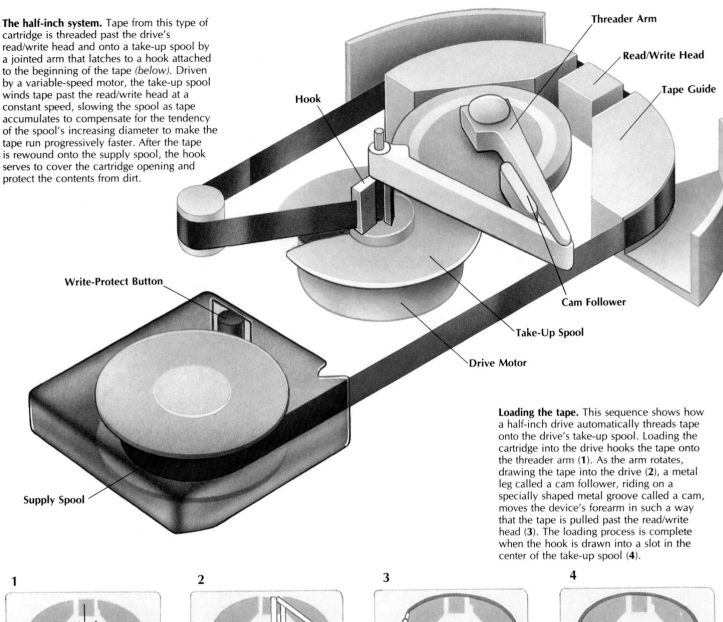

Threader Arm

Read/Write Head

Tape Guide

Hook

Cam Follower

Take-Up Spool

Drive Motor

Write-Protect Button

Supply Spool

Loading the tape. This sequence shows how a half-inch drive automatically threads tape onto the drive's take-up spool. Loading the cartridge into the drive hooks the tape onto the threader arm (**1**). As the arm rotates, drawing the tape into the drive (**2**), a metal leg called a cam follower, riding on a specially shaped metal groove called a cam, moves the device's forearm in such a way that the tape is pulled past the read/write head (**3**). The loading process is complete when the hook is drawn into a slot in the center of the take-up spool (**4**).

1

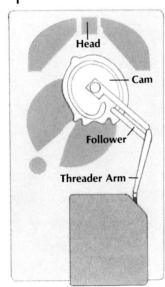

Head

Cam

Follower

Threader Arm

2

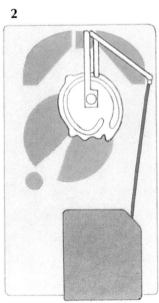

3

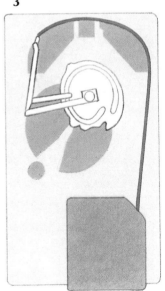

4

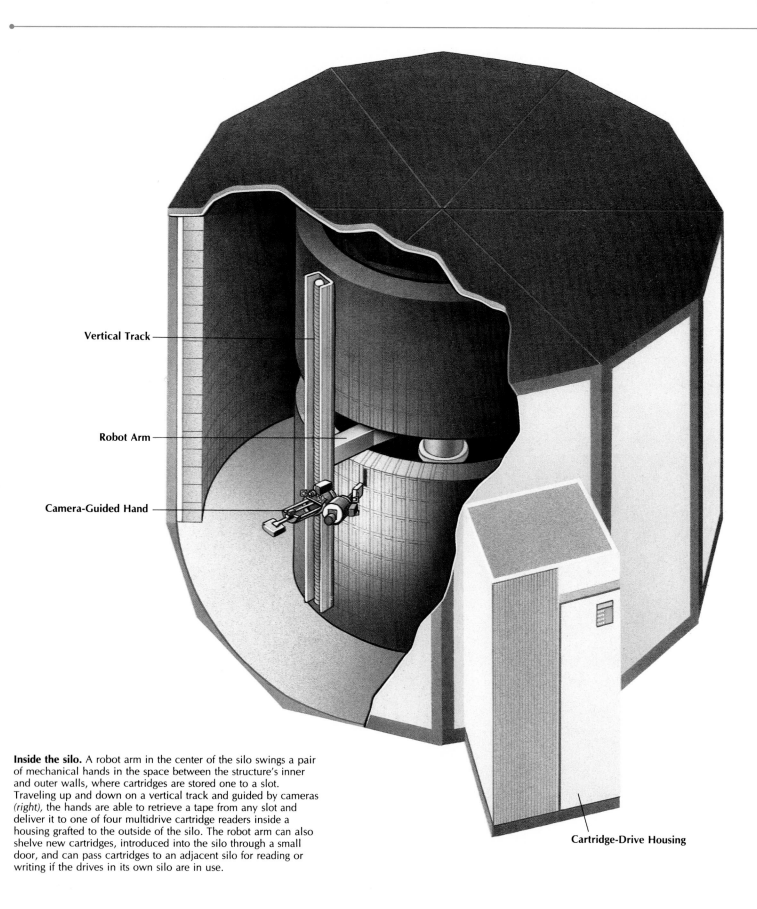

Vertical Track

Robot Arm

Camera-Guided Hand

Cartridge-Drive Housing

Inside the silo. A robot arm in the center of the silo swings a pair of mechanical hands in the space between the structure's inner and outer walls, where cartridges are stored one to a slot. Traveling up and down on a vertical track and guided by cameras *(right)*, the hands are able to retrieve a tape from any slot and deliver it to one of four multidrive cartridge readers inside a housing grafted to the outside of the silo. The robot arm can also shelve new cartridges, introduced into the silo through a small door, and can pass cartridges to an adjacent silo for reading or writing if the drives in its own silo are in use.

A Robot Librarian for Cartridges

Once committed to a reel or cartridge of tape, computer data is often stored off-line, shelved in a library. Filling a request for information from an extensive tape collection can take the librarian—even one who uses roller skates—several minutes or more first to locate the tape and then to carry it from the shelf to the drive.

The automated cartridge library shown here reduces retrieval time to an average of eleven seconds. Such a system offers what some data-processing professionals call near-line storage, which is a compromise between hardware-intensive, on-line storage provided by disks or by tapes already loaded into drives and glacially slow off-line storage. The concen-

tric storage shelves of the "silo" illustrated at left hold approximately 6,000 of the half-inch tape cartridges shown on page 67. At 200 megabytes per cartridge, each silo can store 1,200 gigabytes of data. Moreover, sixteen such silos can be linked into a super system with a capacity of 96,000 tapes, or 19,200 gigabytes.

Each silo is controlled by a computer that directs the two hands of the robot arm inside to the appropriate tape. The arm delivers the tape to one of four readers, each equipped with two to four cartridge drives. Besides offering faster access to data than do conventional tape libraries, this system, per megabyte of data, costs significantly less to operate.

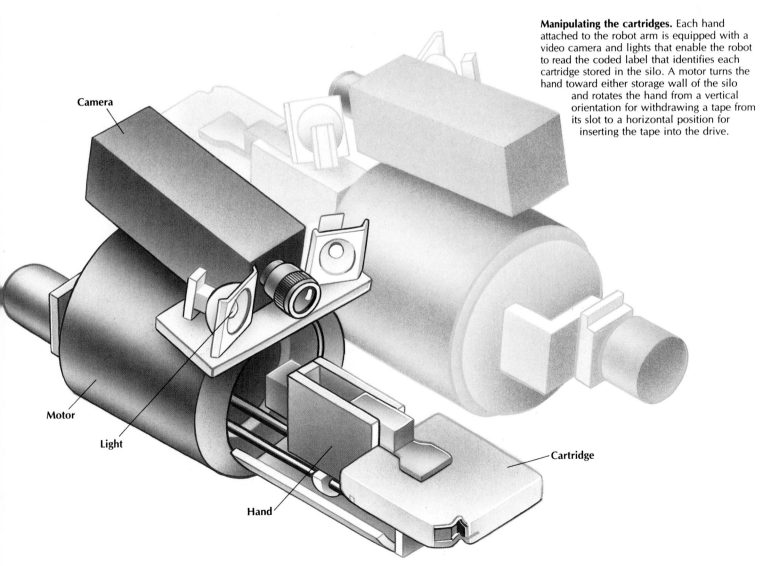

Manipulating the cartridges. Each hand attached to the robot arm is equipped with a video camera and lights that enable the robot to read the coded label that identifies each cartridge stored in the silo. A motor turns the hand toward either storage wall of the silo and rotates the hand from a vertical orientation for withdrawing a tape from its slot to a horizontal position for inserting the tape into the drive.

Camera

Motor

Light

Hand

Cartridge

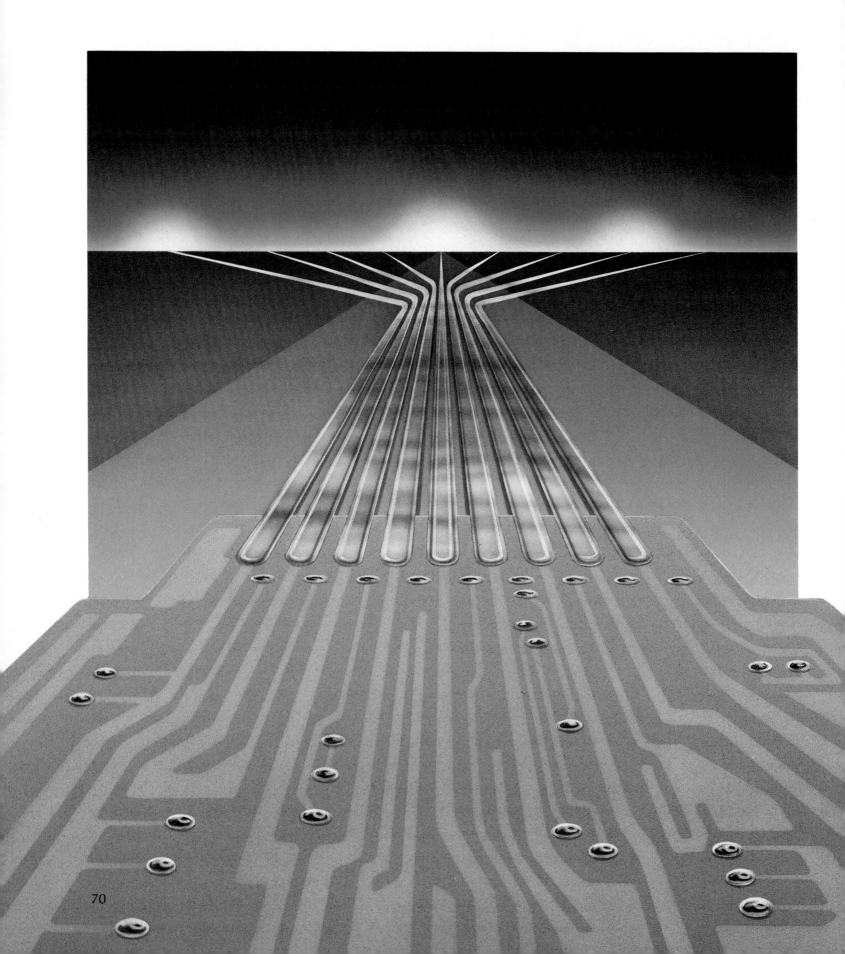

Handling a Flood
of Information

The police did not have much to go on that August day in 1985, merely the images of three fingerprints they had lifted from a stolen Toyota station wagon. The car had been found in Los Angeles near the scene of an attack by the notorious Night Stalker, a serial killer believed to have been responsible for fifteen murders that had occurred during the preceding seven months. Understandably, solving the case had acquired top priority.

It was conceivable that a match for the prints found on the abandoned car might be filed among the fingerprint records of the Los Angeles Police Department. But without an inkling of whom the prints might belong to, there was no way to identify the owner except by comparing them with the fingerprints on the 1.7 million cards in police files, a hopeless undertaking.

On a long shot, the law officers turned for help to the California Department of Justice in Sacramento. At that time, the department was installing a $22.5-million computerized fingerprint-identification system developed by Japan's NEC Corporation. The system boasted eight megabytes of memory, and its array of twenty-three disk drives offered 27.6 gigabytes of storage. A fraction of that storage space held the digital equivalents of fingerprints from 380,000 convicted felons, parolees, and others deemed likely to commit crimes.

To help the Los Angeles police, state officials decided to give the system a trial run, though it was not yet fully operational. Responding to the urgency of the situation, four programmers worked all night to prepare the computer, as photographs of the fingerprints that police hoped would identify the Night Stalker were flown to Sacramento. In the morning, the clearest image was placed under a scanner. The scanner determined the locations of key characteristics known as points of minutiae—places where a fingerprint ridge line ends or forks. (Typically, a fingerprint will have close to 150 points of minutiae.) This information was sent to the system's computer in digital form. Programmers then instructed the computer to select from the multitude of prints on file the ten examples that most closely resembled the one in question. A technician punched a key to launch the search, and groups of fingerprints began flashing from the system's disk drives to the computer, where they were compared with the details scanned from the photograph at the rate of 800 prints per second.

Scant minutes after the search began, identification numbers for ten individuals flickered onto the computer screen, each followed by a numerical score that might range from 0 to 9,999. This number gauges the likelihood that one of the fingerprints selected by the system matched the print found near the scene of the attack. The highest score that appeared was 4,300, more than four times that of the runner-up. "We knew immediately that we had our man," said Elton Johnson, regional manager for NEC's West Coast operations. The finger that had left its mark on the Toyota belonged to Richard Ramirez, a twenty-five-year-old drifter with a record of drug and auto-theft arrests. Ramirez was taken into custody in East Los Angeles the next day.

OF MEMORY AND MINUTIAE

The prowess of the NEC system derives from several design features. Custom circuits accelerate the computer's central processor, while innovative software helps identify even a distorted or blurred print. Most important of all, however, is the ability of the computer and its complement of storage devices to shift quickly in and out of the computer's memory almost unimaginable numbers of points of minutiae. When completed in 1986, the California system had on file the fingerprints of no fewer than five million people. The system thus had to store the details of more than seven billion points of minutiae, as well as the relationships among them.

Fingerprint-identification systems are just one highly specialized example of a huge class of computer applications known as data bases—computerized files of information on practically any subject imaginable, from bank transactions to high-tech research literature. Data bases have blossomed in response to what computer historian David Burnham terms "the natural human instinct to desire more information about everything." Although all computer applications, from the number-crunching requirements encountered in the study of high-energy physics to the production of form letters by word-processing programs, demand at least modest amounts of memory and storage, data bases hunger ceaselessly for these commodities.

Every modern data base has a structure, a framework in which the information is arranged. But before the data-base concept was introduced in the early 1960s—along with the necessary software, called a data-base management system—information storage tended to be fragmented, a state of affairs rife with inefficiencies. In a business, for example, different departments might have to keep computerized files of identical information. A billing department and a catalog-mailing department would each require a mailing list, although both lists would contain the names and addresses of many of the same customers. Not only did data redundancy of this kind waste the time of those employees who had to maintain the files; it also raised the odds that conflicting data might be recorded in each of the separate files. Furthermore, duplicate information squandered precious storage space.

Data-base management systems swept aside these problems by making computers capable of meshing previously discrete files. Such management systems fall into three broad categories: hierarchical, network, and relational (pages 79-81). Each type of data-base management system is defined by the manner in which it establishes relationships between chunks of information. It is the nature of these linkages, rather than the sheer size of memory and storage available, that makes a particular data base easy to use.

The earliest type of data-base management system arranged information in a hierarchy. As in a family tree, data at the top of the hierarchy is accessible only by a single path through the levels below it. In a hierarchical data base containing encyclopedia entries, for example, the only way to reach the desired information might be to specify the initial letter of an entry to narrow the search to a single volume and then spell out the full title to find the entry and display the text. Consulting a cross-reference located in another volume would entail returning to the bottom of the hierarchy. Without question, the hierarchical arrangement eased the retrieval of information, but the lack of horizontal routes between branches of the hierarchy left unresolved the issue of data redundancy and wasted disk space.

A modification of the hierarchical data base, called a network, established the horizontal links missing from its predecessor. Each entry in a network model of the encyclopedia data base could offer direct access to cross-references—provided, of course, that the data-base designer had thought to include all such interconnections between volumes.

Network data bases might have solved the data-redundancy problem, had they only been easier to design and use. A diagram of a complicated networked data base might well be described as byzantine—logical, perhaps, but incomprehensible to all but the expert.

In the early 1970s, an IBM researcher by the name of Edgar F. Codd touched data redundancy with a kind of magic wand, and the problem all but disappeared. Codd, a graduate of Oxford University in England, had co-authored a streamlined error-correction code for IBM's Selective Sequence Electronic Calculator shortly after he was hired by the company in 1949. Later he brought multiprogramming—a technique that allows a computer to alternately execute portions of several programs—to IBM's first supercomputer, which the company called Stretch.

Codd disposed of data redundancy with an organizational strategy that evolved from his work on set theory, a branch of mathematics that deals with relationships among groups of numbers. Codd called his approach a relational data base, and its adaptability and ease of use brought the scheme instant acclaim from programmers.

Unlike the hierarchical and network systems, which require that all possible routes to information be defined explicitly when the data base is set up, a relational data base contains many implicit links between files. No longer need an encyclopedia browser be concerned that some cross-references might be missing. Instead, the reader could request the data-base management system itself to unveil interconnections that the user suspected might exist between entries. In finding those links, Codd's system automatically uncovers useful relationships at the moment the information is requested, revealing hidden webs of cross-referencing on demand.

INFORMATION, PLEASE

Ease of use combined with the conservation of storage space inherent in Codd's system and its derivatives kicked the growth and proliferation of data bases into high gear. Though data bases originated to serve the in-house needs of business, government, and other institutions, the concept has broadened since then to embrace more commercial applications. The most popular—and the most profitable—of these publicly accessible data bases is the computerized information bank, which brings together masses of data from such sources as books, journals, and magazines that in the past could be examined only one by one. The information bank holds the documents in readiness on direct-access disks and for a fee, retrieves relevant portions of them according to a kind of master index to all the information on hand. These electronic libraries have multiplied so rapidly—there are several thousand worldwide—that separate data bases have been established just to keep track of them.

Memory Unlimited

Computer programs and data commonly expand to overflow the memory available to them. Sophisticated computer operating systems solve this problem with a technique called virtual memory, which uses special hardware—often including a speedy hard-disk drive having an access time of only a few milliseconds—to create the illusion of limitless memory in the computer.

To achieve this effect, a virtual-memory operating system divides programs and data into sections and stores them on disk. Then, instead of transferring an entire program and its

Beyond the horizon. To a computer programmer or someone using the machine, virtual memory appears boundless. Programs *(light-colored blocks)* and their associated data *(darker blocks)* fit comfortably here, even though they would easily exceed the capacity of the computer's real memory *(far right)*.

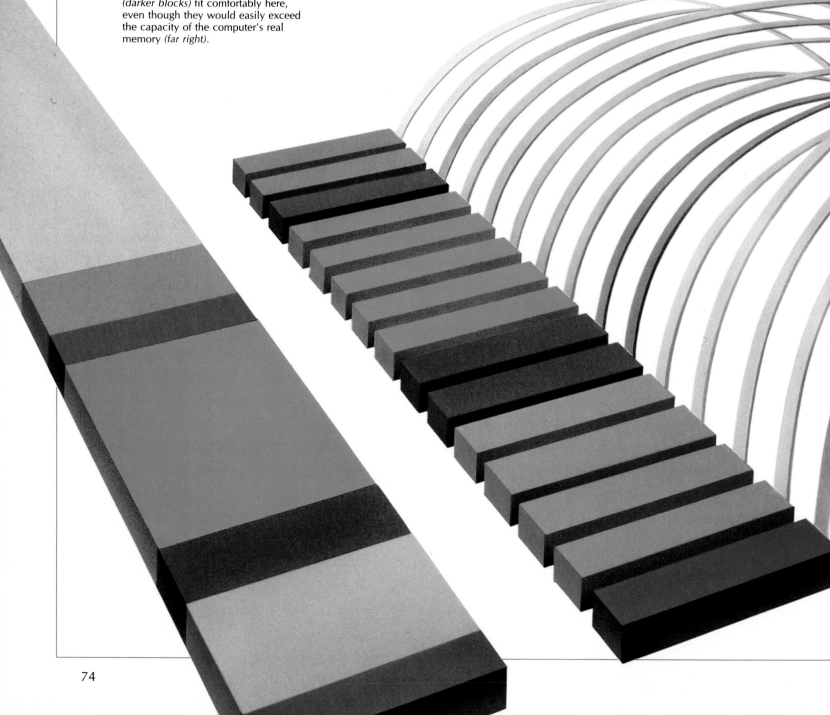

data into memory for execution, the operating system loads only those portions that are needed at the outset. As additional sections are required, they are automatically swapped from the disk into memory. Inactive sections in memory are overwritten to make room for new arrivals.

The advantages of this arrangement are manifold. Programmers need not worry about their work outgrowing the computer's memory; they are free to add features and conveniences as they wish. Software can be written without regard for its location in real memory. A virtual-memory system ensures both that a program can find its own components wherever they may be stored and that software never impermissibly takes over memory that is already occupied, perhaps by the operating system itself. From the computer owner's point of view, virtual memory increases the utility of expensive hardware, allowing the central processing unit (CPU) to take advantage of pauses in one program to perform tasks in another. Rather than executing a single program held completely in memory, the CPU may have access to the active sections of a dozen or more.

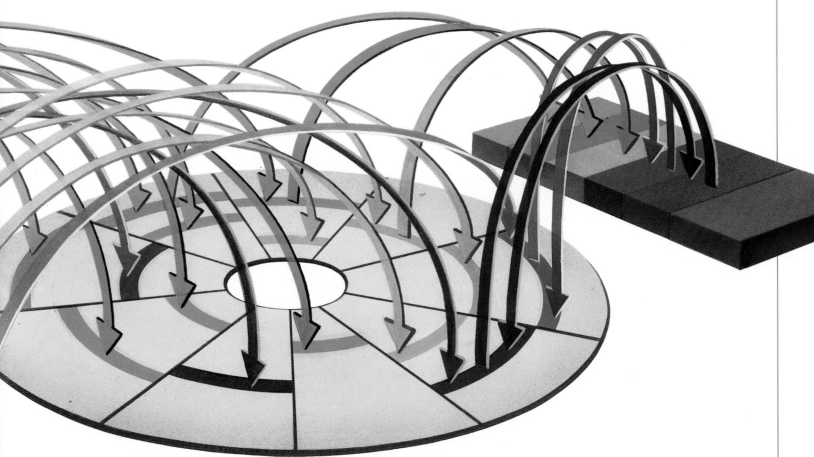

Storing sections. When entered in a virtual-memory system, each program and data file is sliced into pieces. In the scheme shown at left, the pieces, called pages, are equal in size (not the case with all systems). As a rule, data and programs are assigned to different pages; if a slice of either does not fill a page, the leftover space remains blank. The operating system then loads each page onto the disk *(above)* wherever space is available and creates an index to the pages and their locations.

Retrieving pages. When a virtual-memory page not in memory is needed, the operating system *(red)* fetches it from the disk. In memory, each page has bits—called flags—that indicate whether the section has been used recently and whether the contents have been modified. At regular intervals, the operating system scans the memory. Pages that have not been used since the preceding scan are slated as available for overwriting. Before the space is reused, a flag is checked to see whether the page has been altered. If so, it is rewritten to the disk with the modifications *(double arrows)*.

The array of data bases is a dizzying one, ranging from Agnet, which provides crop prices and other kinds of information that are vital to farmers, to the ZIP Code Demographic Data Base, which stores the statistics on deaths, births, marriages, and the like in 35,000 postal zones throughout the United States. Financial information has the broadest currency overall; nearly half of the electronic data that is sold in the United States pertains to stock-market and commodity-market transactions.

As data bases have grown, the storage-space savings that resulted from the relational structure have been gobbled up by ever-increasing amounts of information. In this, computers obey an information-age corollary of Parkinson's Law: "Data expands to fill the space available to hold it."

Other applications can be even more voracious than data bases. Computer-generated spaceship battles featured in the 1984 movie *The Last Starfighter,* for example, required so much memory space—24 million bits to digitize the elements of a single color frame—that a Cray X-MP supercomputer was called in to produce the sequences. Though capable of processing one billion bits per second, the Cray nonetheless required an entire month to complete the film's twenty-five minutes of combat footage. Nor do those figures represent the high end of the scale; to convincingly re-create human rather than inanimate forms demands even greater memory capacity.

SPACE-SAVING TOOLS

Answering the never-ending public clamor for more memory and storage is not always practical—or even possible. When such circumstances occur, programmers have devised techniques that get the most use out of existing memory and storage space. The labels of a number of these software stratagems—data compression, purging, garbage collection—offer a clue to the kinds of service the techniques perform.

Data compression, a family of related techniques, helps to reduce the amount of memory or storage space that information needs to occupy. To accomplish this, the number of bits—ones and zeros—used to communicate information to the computer must be reduced. One obstacle to such an abridgment is the rigid data-encoding scheme called ASCII (American Standard Code for Information Interchange), which requires that a string of eight bits be used as a representation of every individual "character" in a data file. ASCII furnishes 128 unique combinations of ones and zeros, each of which stands for a numeral, a letter, a mathematical or other special symbol, or a formatting character such as a space or a carriage return.

Such provision is overly generous, however, because there are few data files that require all 128 combinations. For example, in a spreadsheet, a tool that is widely used for financial analysis, the primary need is for just ten distinguishable combinations, representing the numerals 0 through 9. With such a small number of characters to accommodate, the spreadsheet is an excellent candidate for compression. Using a set of rules, or an algorithm, known as a compressor-expander—a "compander," in programmers' parlance—a data-compression program translates each numeral from its ASCII code of eight bits into a four-bit code, which allows for sixteen unique combinations and yields a memory- and storage-space saving of 50 percent.

Similar means can condense labels in spreadsheets or other text files, which likewise have no need for all the characters available in ASCII. The alphabet requires fifty-two ASCII binary combinations—twenty-six for lowercase letters and twenty-six for capitals—while the symbols for italics, boldface, punctuation, and so on consume only about a dozen more. Thus every element of the text file can be represented as a string of only six bits, which offer sixty-four unique combinations. This translates into a 25-percent saving in disk space over ASCII coding. Usually, there is no saving in memory. Because the central processors of most computers do not handle data in six-bit units or multiples thereof, this kind of encoding is usually reconverted into eight-bit bytes when a file is loaded into memory for processing.

The same thing is true of an often-applied process called Huffman coding, which nearly doubles the economy achieved by the six-bit method. Invented in 1952 by David A. Huffman, a doctoral candidate in engineering at Massachusetts Institute of Technology (M.I.T.), this method of data compression takes the approach of assigning short codes to the characters that appear most often in a textual passage and longer codes to the less common characters. In the English language, both the space between words and the letter e, for example, are assigned three-bit codes by the computer before the data is stored. The eight next most common letters receive four-bit codes, and so on. Typically, a Huffman-coded document in English occupies about 48 percent less space on a disk than does the identical information coded in ASCII.

Compression can serve the cause of computer graphics even more effectively than it does text. A picture on a computer screen is generated by an electron beam scanning each of the screen's horizontal lines as many as sixty times per second. The beam changes the color of the pixels—the thousands of individually lighted dotlike picture elements that make up the screen—in accordance with numbers stored in a data file for each of the images. On a monochrome screen, the beam either lights up a pixel in response to a stored one or leaves the pixel dark in response to a stored zero.

Before the sequence of ones and zeros representing an image is committed to disk, however, it is analyzed by a compander that abbreviates the bit stream in accordance with certain rules. The compander replaces strings of identical bits (which are those that represent a line of uniform color in the image) with a short symbol—"Repeat sixty-four zeros," for example—that is then recorded on the disk. When the disk is read, its output passes back through the compander, which reconverts the short symbol into its unabridged sequence of bits. Such a procedure can reduce the disk space that is needed to store monochrome pictures by 90 percent or more. Full-color images may be compressed the same way; but since these contain fewer strings of identical bits, they do not benefit quite so dramatically.

Data compression has demonstrated its worth most conclusively in space applications, where it serves to reduce the amount of information that a deep-space probe must transmit across the vastness of space. Scientists of the National Aeronautics and Space Administration availed themselves of the technique to retrieve vividly detailed images of the planet Uranus during the flyby of the *Voyager 2* in 1986, then in 1989 gathered a wealth of equally prized information about Neptune, using the same strategy.

OF PURGATIVES AND GARBAGE COLLECTION

Where memory or storage cannot be conserved by data compression, purging can help. This space-saving approach grew out of disgruntlement with computer time-sharing systems. Time-sharing was hailed as a watershed in computer processing when it appeared in the late 1950s. Through the expedient of a master program called a supervisor or an executive, a time-sharing computer could run several programs at once, cycling through them in round-robin fashion by devoting a brief burst of processing time to each in turn.

Time-sharing allowed several people at the same time to run independent programs on the same computer—and hence draw simultaneously on the computer's memory. Within two decades, however, even mainframe computers were hard pressed to accommodate the proliferant legions of time-sharers and their competing demands for computer memory.

In response, software engineers have devised schemes to free memory space by automatically erasing, or purging, data that has become obsolete. The Cray Time-Sharing System at the University of California's Supercomputer Center in Livermore, for example, is programmed to purge memory of any data and programs that have not been reviewed or altered during the last thirty hours— eighty hours over weekends. Memory contents in the time-sharing system contain an embedded code, called the "time of last reference," that acts as a digital telltale: The reference code alerts the computer that an area of memory has stood idle long enough to be purged, and the file is then erased from the computer. (This approach proved to have certain risks, however: On one occasion, important data was lost when the system's operators neglected to extend the computer's time of last reference to account for the occurrence in the work schedule of a four-day holiday weekend.)

Garbage collection is a similar approach to the problem of stale data. This technique originated as a feature of the programming language LISP (for LISt Processing). Conceived by mathematician John McCarthy at M.I.T. in 1958, LISP was designed for applications in the memory-intensive field of artificial intelligence. The language itself is a conspicuous consumer of memory, for it deals in high-level symbolic expressions rather than in numbers that can be easily converted to binary code; and these symbols are recorded in machine-usable form as rather bulky lists. As a LISP program runs, it calls the lists into memory one after another, inexorably filling the machine's finite memory to capacity. In the absence of any means to reclaim some of that memory space, the list needed next by the program could not be brought into the computer, and the machine would simply cease operating.

To keep things moving, McCarthy introduced a software refinement to identify the memory locations, or cells, where lists reside that have become superfluous to the program being run. The garbage collector then empties the lists from those cells, allowing the program to resume operation.

Originally, the computer operator had to initiate garbage collection, but the process was soon made automatic, a source of amusement when garbage collection was unveiled before a blue-ribbon audience attending a university symposium at M.I.T. in the early 1960s. McCarthy later recalled that the demonstration was proceeding on schedule when suddenly the computer's output device—a typewriterlike piece of equipment in those days before CRT moni-

Filing Strategies for Computer Data

Storing information randomly in a computer, like stuffing papers into a drawer, is nearly useless as a record-keeping technique. Filing cabinets keep papers organized. In computers, the job of imposing order falls to software known generically as a data-base management system (DBMS).

All DBMS's store information as records, in effect electronic forms that are filled out with facts about a person, place, event—anything that anyone might wish to keep a file of. But how one DBMS stores records and retrieves them on demand may differ significantly from the method used by another. Some store information in a hierarchy that resembles an in-

verted family tree. Others establish links between the various levels in a hierarchy to form a structure called a network. Perhaps the most widely used systems employ something that data-base professionals call a relational arrangement. The illustrations on this and the following pages show the major differences between these three methods as applied to a much-simplified data base, such as a florist might find helpful when stocking a shop.

In a hierarchical data base *(below)*, records at one level are accessible only through the records at levels above them. Thus, to retrieve information from the depths of such a data base, a computer operator must be intimately familiar with the structure of the trees, a formidable requirement when the data base is large and complex. Furthermore, because there are no cross-links between trees, data applicable to more than one of them must be repeated, a feature of this kind of data base that makes it somewhat profligate with storage space.

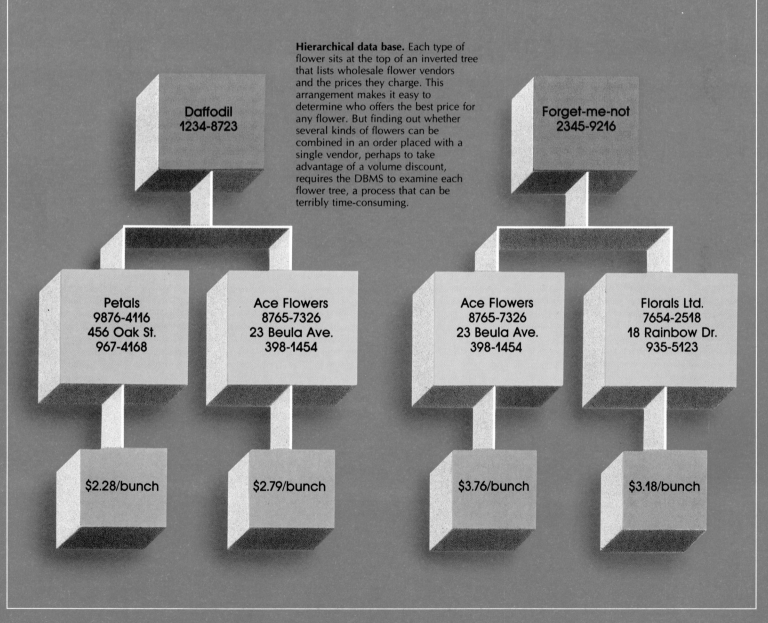

Hierarchical data base. Each type of flower sits at the top of an inverted tree that lists wholesale flower vendors and the prices they charge. This arrangement makes it easy to determine who offers the best price for any flower. But finding out whether several kinds of flowers can be combined in an order placed with a single vendor, perhaps to take advantage of a volume discount, requires the DBMS to examine each flower tree, a process that can be terribly time-consuming.

Daffodil
1234-8723

Forget-me-not
2345-9216

Petals
9876-4116
456 Oak St.
967-4168

Ace Flowers
8765-7326
23 Beula Ave.
398-1454

Ace Flowers
8765-7326
23 Beula Ave.
398-1454

Florals Ltd.
7654-2518
18 Rainbow Dr.
935-5123

$2.28/bunch

$2.79/bunch

$3.76/bunch

$3.18/bunch

Alternatives to a Hierarchy

The rigidity of a hierarchical structure can be overcome by providing horizontal links between records. Two very different approaches to this goal are represented in network and relational data bases.

A network data base bears a resemblance to the hierarchical model, but there is an important difference: Any record can be linked to any other. This flexibility makes the network structure superior to a hierarchy for retrieving information that may cross hierarchical boundaries. As versatile as this approach may be, however, it complicates the process of retrieving information. Even more than a hierarchichal data base, a network data base places a premium on the operator's understanding the structure of the data, which can become so complex that only specially trained individuals are able to navigate successfully through it.

The relational data-base structure offers a much simpler way to extract information from computer files. In this arrangement, data is listed in tables, each row of which con-

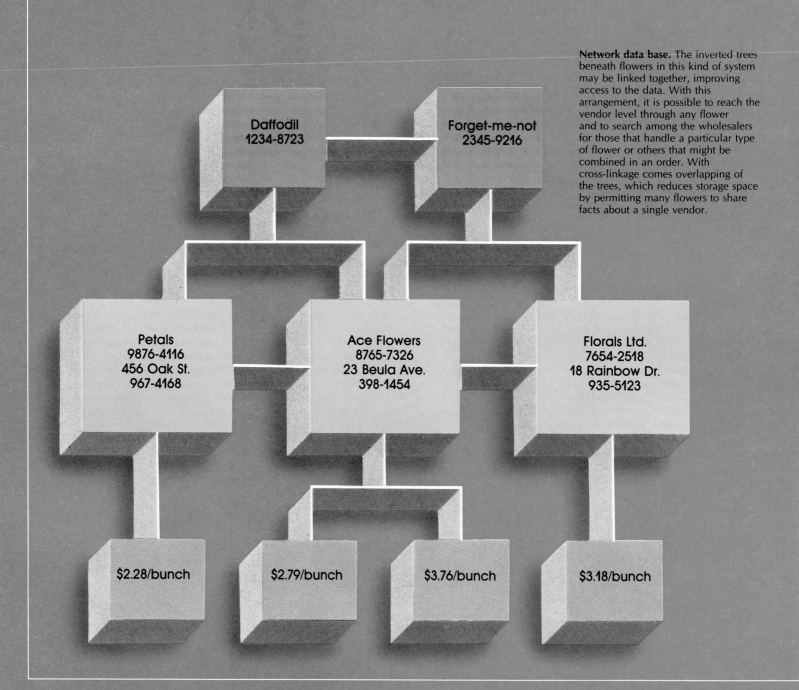

Network data base. The inverted trees beneath flowers in this kind of system may be linked together, improving access to the data. With this arrangement, it is possible to reach the vendor level through any flower and to search among the wholesalers for those that handle a particular type of flower or others that might be combined in an order. With cross-linkage comes overlapping of the trees, which reduces storage space by permitting many flowers to share facts about a single vendor.

Daffodil
1234-8723

Forget-me-not
2345-9216

Petals
9876-4116
456 Oak St.
967-4168

Ace Flowers
8765-7326
23 Beula Ave.
398-1454

Florals Ltd.
7654-2518
18 Rainbow Dr.
935-5123

$2.28/bunch

$2.79/bunch

$3.76/bunch

$3.18/bunch

stitutes a record. A column from one table can be included in others, forging a link between all the tables in which the column appears. The advantage is that a computer operator need only be familiar with the information stored in the data base—not its structure—in order to query the data base successfully. In the sample relational data base at right, the Vendor Number column is included not only in the Vendor Table but in the Cost Table as well. When a query is submitted that relates to vendors, the DBMS automatically retrieves data from both of the tables, when appropriate, even though the individual who is asking the question may have no idea that they are related.

Relational data base. Here, florist information is stored as rows in tables of data—one for flowers, one for vendors, a third for costs. Rather than forming a hierarchy, the tables are peers, accessible either directly or through each other. In response to a request for all data about daffodils, for example, the DBMS finds the flower's identification number in the Flower Table and looks to that column in the Cost Table, and from there to the vendor-number column of the Vendor Table. Data from all three tables is compiled and displayed (bottom).

Flower Table

Flower Name	Flower ID
Daffodil	1234-8723
Forget-me-not	2345-9216

Vendor Table

Vendor Number	Name	Address	Phone
9876-4116	Petals	456 Oak St.	967-4168
8765-7326	Ace Flowers	23 Beula Ave.	398-1454
7654-2518	Florals Ltd.	18 Rainbow Dr.	935-5123

Cost Table

Vendor Number	Flower ID	Price
9876-4116	1234-8723	$2.28/bunch
8765-7326	1234-8723	$2.79/bunch
8765-7326	2345-9216	$3.76/bunch
7654-2518	2345-9216	$3.18/bunch

Results

Vendor Number	Name	Address	Phone	Flower ID	Price
9876-4116	Petals	456 Oak St.	967-4168	1234-8723	$2.28/ bunch
8765-7326	Ace Flowers	23 Beula Ave.	398-1454	2345-9216	$2.79/ bunch

tors—clacked out a message: "The garbage collector has been called." The program was merely signaling to the operators that certain lists were about to be dumped from memory; no one in the audience had ever encountered a garbage collector in a computer, however, and as the attendees read the message they dissolved in laughter. "I think some of them thought we were victims of a practical joker," McCarthy concluded.

Garbage collection remains a key feature of programs written in computer languages such as Prolog and LISP, which are tailored for artificial intelligence. Such software frequently owes its effectiveness to rapid garbage-collection techniques. A measure of the tactic's continuing vitality is the fact that a large LISP program may spend 10 to 30 percent of its execution time in the process of collecting garbage.

LOGICAL LEGERDEMAIN

Perhaps the handiest memory-management tool of all is virtual memory, an electronic sleight of hand that appears to increase the size of a computer's memory without actually doing so. It determines which parts of a program or which pieces of data must reside in active memory and which parts may be temporarily relegated to storage.

Such partitioning is called for because a computer can execute only those instructions that reside in its memory. Yet many computer programs are too large to fit in the memory space available, so they must be split into smaller portions that can then be shunted in and out of memory as needed. This painstaking task of slicing a program, called overlaying, originally fell to computer programmers. The job required a programmer not only to keep track of the memory location of every program parcel (lest the next section loaded into memory unexpectedly overwrite parts of another), but to ensure that interdependent program components were always present in memory at the same time. The opportunity for error was abundant, even in relatively simple programs. By the late 1960s, software had grown so complex that the process of overlaying had grown to consume as much as 40 percent of the time that programmers devoted to their work.

The British computer scientist Tom Kilburn, who in the mid-1940s had helped conceive Williams-tube memory, was determined to automate this chore in a powerful computer that he and a team of Manchester University computer scientists began to develop in 1956. The design for the computer, to be called the Atlas I, specified a 16,000-word ferrite-core memory—too small, in Kilburn's view. Casting about for a way to expand this capacity without increasing the number of cores, which his budget strictly limited, Kilburn thought of linking the core memory to a much larger and less expensive storage system—in essence, a secondary memory—that consisted of magnetic drums that were equipped with a total capacity of 96,000 words.

When the Atlas I was completed in 1959, a special software feature called a swapping algorithm directed traffic between the computer's memory and storage. Kilburn's algorithm divided a computer program into sections of 512 computer words each, called pages, and then, almost magically, these pages were shuttled between core memory and the drums as necessary to execute the program's instructions. Whenever a computer program requested a word from a page that was not at that moment residing in memory—a situation known as a page fault—a special instruction suspended the program's execution until the page containing the sought-after word had been retrieved from the storage drum. Furthermore, the algorithm placed the page in a memory location where it would not interfere with other parts of the program or with other tasks that the computer might be engaged in.

Kilburn's innovative use of a computer's storage capacity as a direct extension of memory came to be known as virtual memory, because it had the effect of increasing the amount of the computer's memory. Although the business of page-swapping did consume valuable processing time, Kilburn's software made it possible for machines with a small internal memory to run large programs; it also permitted computer memory to be distributed efficiently among the various users of a time-sharing system. And one of the technique's most welcome attributes of all was that virtual memory delivered programmers from the tedious task of overlaying.

The trailblazing Atlas I also introduced the concept of multiprogramming that IBM would later employ in its Stretch supercomputer. By using the time required to respond to one program's page fault as execution time for another program, the Atlas I was able to switch rapidly among diverse tasks. But the innovation brought problems.

In particular, multiprogramming was afflicted with a kind of electronic seizure called thrashing: As segments of more and more programs vied for space in the computer's real memory, the system came to the point where it spent more time switching parts of programs in and out of memory than it did executing program instructions. Computer historian Peter Denning has likened this thrashing to the circumstances of office workers besieged by so many different tasks they "spend all their time shuffling papers and no time doing real work." To keep thrashing at bay, software designers wrote routines that automatically bumped one or more competing programs from memory until the system had a chance to satisfy the conflicting requests.

KILBURN'S LEGACY
Although Kilburn and his collaborators built only three Atlas I machines, the idea of virtual memory spread rapidly during the early 1960s. In California, for example, the Atlas I inspired the Burroughs adding-machine company to assemble a twenty-five-member team to design a virtual-memory computer of its own. The Burroughs group was remarkable in at least two respects. From the outset, it included software specialists—a rare practice at a time when most computer manufacturers brought in the programming experts only after the hardware designers had dictated what the machine's specifications would be. Second, the team boasted more than the usual quota of brains. Six of the group's software engineers were "outrageous geniuses," recalled project manager William Lonergan. "There was a white heat in the air."

That white heat forged the highly advanced Burroughs B5000. Completed in 1963, the machine featured a version of Kilburn's virtual memory. As with the Atlas I, the inclusion of virtual memory made it possible for the B5000 to offer multiprogramming. Burroughs' competitors would require a decade to duplicate the memory-management scheme of the B5000. At IBM, for example, problems with both software and hardware delayed the successful introduction of virtual memory until 1972, when the company offered it as a key element in its System/370 series of computers.

Since then, virtual memory has continued to find widespread use, figuring prominently in the architectures of mainframes, minicomputers, and even microcomputers. In advanced engineering workstations, for example, virtual memory coupled with multiprogramming makes it possible for an engineer to have the computer simultaneously perform a complicated structural analysis, create a drawing of another project, and calculate a spreadsheet—and then display all three activities in different areas of a computer screen.

TOWARD INFINITE CAPACITY

While some designers devise and refine techniques for creating the illusion of ample memory, others attempt to meet head on the demand for greater capacity. The continuing decline in the price of memory chips makes feasible a strategy in which computer engineers beef up primary memory by stuffing a machine full of chips. At Princeton University during the 1980s, two professors of computer science named Richard J. Lipton and Hector Garcia-Molina and their associates began building what they called a Massive Memory Machine, or M3, to solve memory-intensive calculations in the fields of data-base management, artificial intelligence, and integrated-circuit design. When the M3 was completed in 1989, its main memory contained 10,000 chips, each able to accommodate about 100 kilobytes, or 100,000 bytes, of data. The M3's memory thus held a gigabyte of information—one billion characters, or more than half a million pages of text.

Computer memories the size of the M3's hardly threaten to make memory-management tactics obsolete, however. Like their predecessors, gigabyte memories and their kin may soon be filled to overflowing by applications that are even more ravening of data than those in existence. In anticipation of that day, computer scientists have begun to consider an alternative storage technology that archives computer information as bytes of light.

Coping with Wayward 0s and 1s

Error is a fact of life for computers. Whenever data is transmitted or wherever it is stored, it is vulnerable to many different forces and conditions that can physically distort the record, changing 0s into 1s and vice versa. The consequences can be devastating; a single wrong bit can change the meaning of an entire sequence of bits, perhaps throwing off a lengthy mathematical calculation or causing a computer to misinterpret a command.

Luckily, binary information can be effectively protected against the vagaries of an imperfect world. The following pages illustrate only a few strategies in a wide range available to computers for catching errors and correcting them. The principle that lies behind most error detection and correction methods is redundancy; individual groups of data bits have extra information added to them that summarizes the original data. Later, after both the data and its summary have been transmitted or stored, they are compared to see if they still match. If not, the computer can assume that an error has corrupted the information.

Data-summary techniques vary from the ingeniously simple to the cunningly complex, the choice often depending on the nature of the errors expected. Two classes, known as soft errors and hard errors, call for quite different approaches.

Soft errors are temporary faults, caused by signal noise during a transmission, for example, or a low-energy electrical surge, that briefly interfere with the reading or writing of data. The best way to handle them is with a simple and efficient error-detection code that does no more than signal the occurrence of an erroneous bit somewhere among the members of a coded group. Because the error is unlikely to repeat, a retransmission of the data or rereading it from memory or storage usually suffices to repair the damage.

Hard errors, however, are permanent. Individual memory cells can fail through normal wear or because of manufacturing defects. Moreover, disks and tapes can suffer physical damage such as scratches or nicks that unalterably affect the device's ability to store data. But the most sophisticated coding schemes will overcome even permanent defects—by going beyond mere detection to the actual correcting of wrong values. In the end, a computer may resort to a combination of codes to keep its data as safe as possible from the inevitable assault of errors.

An Even-Odd Test for Flagging Errors

The two simplest methods of detecting an error, known as parity check *(below)* and checksum *(opposite)*, share the same basic strategy: They count the number of 1s in a series of bits, then add an extra digit to make the total number of 1s come out even (or odd, in some designs). To confirm that the bits have not changed during transmission or storage, the 1s are recounted; if the result is an odd number, it means that there is an error.

A Special Kind of Addition

The circled plus sign denotes the exclusive-OR function, a standard logic operation in computers that yields either a 0 or a 1 when adding two binary digits. If the two digits match (0 + 0 or 1 + 1), the result is 0; if they differ (0 + 1 or 1 + 0), the answer is 1.

Creating a check bit. A computer works step by step, through seven exclusive-OR additions *(blue brackets),* to calculate the check bit for a byte of data *(yellow).* The two leftmost bits are added first; the result *(lowest red digit)* is then added to the third bit, that result to the fourth, and so on. The final answer of 1 *(right)* means that the original byte contains an odd number of 1s.

Checking for even parity. The check bit and data byte together form a nine-bit string with even parity, or an even number of 1s. To check for error after transmission or storage, the computer applies exclusive-OR addition to all nine bits. If no error has occurred, as in the top example below, the bits add up to a 0 *(white)*—confirmation of even parity. But if a bit has gone bad—in the bottom example, the sixth bit has switched from 1 to 0—the exclusive-OR tally yields a telltale 1, signaling an odd number of 1s and thus an error.

Both systems rely on the exclusive-OR operation *(box, left)* to do their counting of 1s. This operation conveniently labels odd sets of 1s with a 1 and even sets with a 0, so coding is simply a matter of appending these results to the original data. Odd sets automatically become even with the extra 1, and even sets remain unchanged by the extra 0.

Parity and checksum coding work most effectively when the errors are few and far between. If there are two errors within a group of bits that share a parity bit, the number of 1s will remain even and the errors will go undetected. Furthermore, neither of these methods can correct errors, and neither one of them is adequate when there is a permanent defect in a memory cell or other storage element that makes retransmission ineffective as a remedy. Such situations call for more elaborate coding strategies capable of fixing the problem as well as finding it.

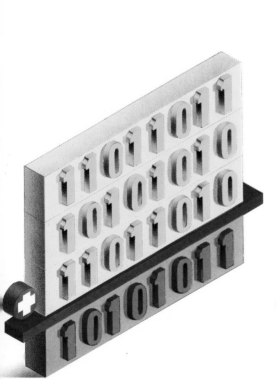
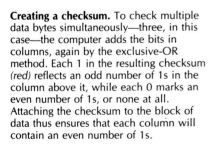

Creating a checksum. To check multiple data bytes simultaneously—three, in this case—the computer adds the bits in columns, again by the exclusive-OR method. Each 1 in the resulting checksum *(red)* reflects an odd number of 1s in the column above it, while each 0 marks an even number of 1s, or none at all. Attaching the checksum to the block of data thus ensures that each column will contain an even number of 1s.

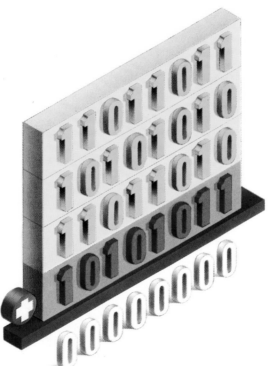

Adding in the checksum. To examine the entire block for error, the computer adds data bytes and checksum together. In the absence of errors, the computer finds an even number of 1s in each column, and exclusive-OR addition produces a perfect string of 0s *(above)*.

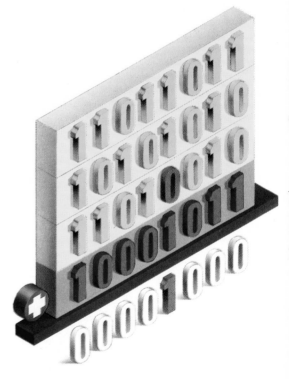

Catching an error. In the example above, a random error in the third byte has changed a 1 to a 0. Exclusive-OR addition now yields a 1 in the fifth position from the left, a sign to the computer that a mistake has occurred somewhere in that column. Unable to identify the error's exact location, the computer must call for a retransmission or must reread the entire block and check it again in the hope that the flaw was temporary.

A Three-Ring Scheme for Data Repair

Because of the inherent, two-state simplicity of binary numbers, a computer can correct an error in a group of bits merely by switching a 0 back to a 1 or vice versa. But first it must find out exactly which of the bits went wrong, and pinpointing the offender calls for more ingenuity than either parity or checksum coding can muster.

The error-correcting scheme illustrated on these and the next two pages is one of a family of techniques called Hamming codes, named for their inventor, Richard Hamming of Bell Labs. These techniques—variously designed to guard

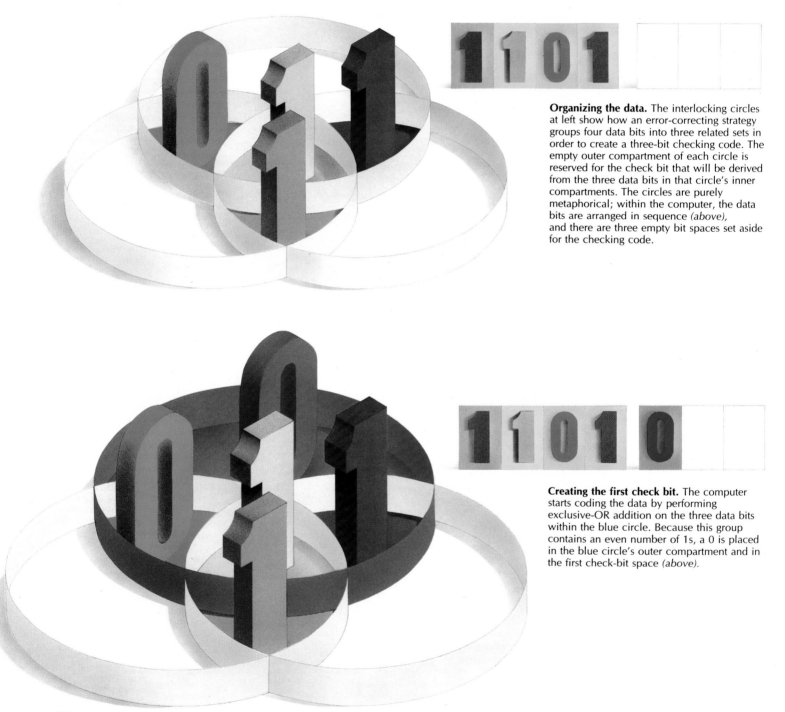

Organizing the data. The interlocking circles at left show how an error-correcting strategy groups four data bits into three related sets in order to create a three-bit checking code. The empty outer compartment of each circle is reserved for the check bit that will be derived from the three data bits in that circle's inner compartments. The circles are purely metaphorical; within the computer, the data bits are arranged in sequence (above), and there are three empty bit spaces set aside for the checking code.

Creating the first check bit. The computer starts coding the data by performing exclusive-OR addition on the three data bits within the blue circle. Because this group contains an even number of 1s, a 0 is placed in the blue circle's outer compartment and in the first check-bit space (above).

different quantities of information—wed data and check bits in cunning logical relationships that identify each bit to the computer. In the version shown here, intended for handling data in four-bit chunks, the relationships are best exemplified by a trio of overlapping, colored circles forming seven different-colored compartments—for the four data and three check bits that make up a coded block.

The basic mechanics are the same as those for parity check and for checksum: exclusive-OR addition of data bits to create a check bit that ensures there will be an even number of 1s overall. But the Hamming code goes through the procedure three times, bringing into play three different combinations of the data bits. The combinations are chosen in such a way that each bit makes a distinctive contribution to the formation of the three check bits. During the checking process *(pages 90-91)*, these differences make it possible for the computer to determine which bit is defective and then fix it on the spot, a facility that helps justify the high price that the Hamming code exacts in memory space—three check bits for every four bits of data.

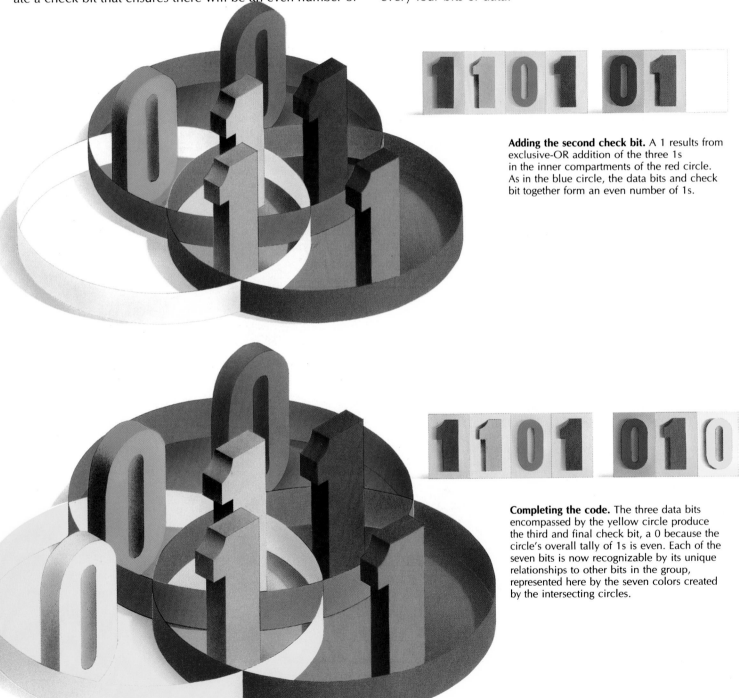

Adding the second check bit. A 1 results from exclusive-OR addition of the three 1s in the inner compartments of the red circle. As in the blue circle, the data bits and check bit together form an even number of 1s.

Completing the code. The three data bits encompassed by the yellow circle produce the third and final check bit, a 0 because the circle's overall tally of 1s is even. Each of the seven bits is now recognizable by its unique relationships to other bits in the group, represented here by the seven colors created by the intersecting circles.

Identifying the Erroneous Bit

Checking a Hamming-coded block, like creating one, entails three separate exclusive-OR calculations—one for each related group, or circle, of bits. Taken on its own, each calculation is a simple parity check, indicating with a 1 or a 0 the presence or absence of an error within that group. But taken together, the answers for the three circles, known as the block's syndrome, enable the computer to establish the precise whereabouts of any single error.

Computing a syndrome. To check for an error, the computer performs exclusive-OR addition on four bits at a time—the three data bits and one check bit within each circle. Since each group should contain an even number of 1s, the answer in each case *(large number outside each circle)* should be a 0. So a pattern, or syndrome, of three 0s indicates that the entire block is error free. The computer confirms this by checking the syndrome against a table listing all eight possible combinations of 0s and 1s that might have occurred *(left)*.

The strategy hinges on the interconnecting relationships built into the code. Because of them, altering any of the seven bits, including the check bits, has a unique effect on the three-bit pattern of 0s and 1s in the syndrome. In the example below, an error in the purple bit creates a one-of-a-kind syndrome because no other bit shares the characteristics of being outside the yellow circle but within both the blue and the red. Had some other bit been wrong, it would have revealed itself by its own distinctive pattern of effects.

Altogether, then, the computer must be able to recognize eight different syndrome patterns, describing eight possible circumstances: no error at all or a single error in any one of the seven bits. A table of syndrome patterns and what the errors signify is stored by the computer. The computer calculates the syndrome, compares it with the table, then fixes any error without further delay.

A telltale pattern. An error that changes the purple bit from 1 to 0 *(striped bit, below)* changes the number of 1s in the blue and red circles but not in the yellow one, and the syndrome bits are affected accordingly: The yellow syndrome stays at 0, reflecting the correct even number of 1s in the yellow circle, while the blue and red syndrome bits change to 1, reflecting the odd tallies within their circles. The table shows that only an error at purple produces a syndrome of 011, and the computer puts things right by changing the purple 0 to a 1.

Extra Protection for Double Trouble

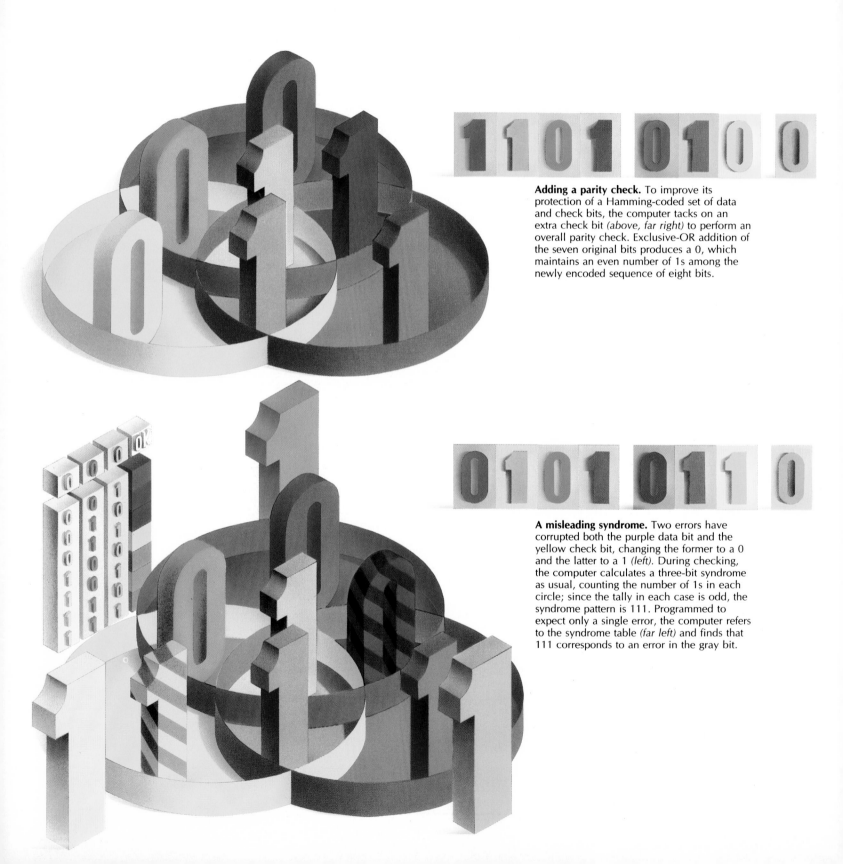

Adding a parity check. To improve its protection of a Hamming-coded set of data and check bits, the computer tacks on an extra check bit *(above, far right)* to perform an overall parity check. Exclusive-OR addition of the seven original bits produces a 0, which maintains an even number of 1s among the newly encoded sequence of eight bits.

A misleading syndrome. Two errors have corrupted both the purple data bit and the yellow check bit, changing the former to a 0 and the latter to a 1 *(left)*. During checking, the computer calculates a three-bit syndrome as usual, counting the number of 1s in each circle; since the tally in each case is odd, the syndrome pattern is 111. Programmed to expect only a single error, the computer refers to the syndrome table *(far left)* and finds that 111 corresponds to an error in the gray bit.

Though a foolproof corrector of single random errors, the Hamming code described on the preceding pages goes haywire in those rare instances when two errors fall within the same encoded block. As the examples below illustrate, in trying to correct what it misinterprets to be a solo mistake, the computer will actually introduce a third error.

To prevent such an event from escaping notice, the Hamming code is often supplemented with the simplest of all coding techniques, an overall parity check *(page 86),* which appends either a 0 or a 1 to make the total number of 1s in a group of bits even. Ironically, the scheme relies on the third error created by the Hamming code; the parity check would miss just two errors, because they would not alter the original even tally of 1s. Once detected, the triple blunder can be remedied only by retransmission, since the coding is insufficient to unerringly identify the two incorrect bits.

Detecting the blunder. Assuming from the first syndrome check that the gray bit is incorrect, the computer changes it from 1 to 0, unwittingly adding a third error *(above).* A new syndrome check is no help, because it produces a misleading all-clear signal of 000. Only by running an overall parity check can the computer discover the damage. Exclusive-OR addition of all eight bits, including the extra check bit, yields a 1 *(left),* indicating that the block no longer contains the proper even number of 1s. Unable to pinpoint the three errors, the computer can do no more than label the entire block as unreliable and request retransmission.

Conquering a Burst of Errors

Although single and even double random errors succumb to the encoding schemes already mentioned, deviations can occur in much larger numbers, affecting whole sequences of adjacent bits. Sudden power fluctuations are often to blame for these so-called burst errors, but scratches on a disk or dust on a read/write head can also wreak this havoc. High-density supercomputer memories and such storage devices as optical disks, where bits are packed as tightly together as possible, are especially vulnerable.

The simplest approach is to use a process known as interleaving, which spreads out errors and makes them manageable. Groups of bits are first assigned parity bits to protect against single errors, then the bits are shuffled in an orderly fashion so that the original groups are broken up and the

10110101 01101001 10100010 11011010 10100101

10111000 01010101 11101111 10010010 01010011

10111000 01010101 111011 10010010 01010011

10110101 01101001 10100010 11011010 10100101

members widely dispersed. If a burst error strikes during transmission, no one group of bits suffers disproportionately; when the bits are reassembled into their original order, errors are distributed among many groups and fall easy prey to the kinds of coding explained on the preceding pages.

Interleaving schemes can be designed to cover error bursts of different lengths; the key is to prevent more than one error from occurring in a single group of bits. In the simple example below, it takes a pattern of sixty-four bits to guard against burst errors up to eight bits long.

01100101 00111001 01101111

Interleaving the bits. Eight bytes of data, each eight bits long *(above)*, are methodically shuffled before transmission to protect against burst errors. The bytes are first written horizontally into a tier of registers *(right)*, starting with the rightmost byte and filling the rows from top to bottom. For transmission, the bytes are read out vertically, from bottom to top and from left to right. Each eight-bit group is now a meaningless jumble *(below)*, made up of one bit from each of the eight bytes.

10001101 00110001 11001111

10001101 00110001 11001111

Restoring the message. During transmission, an error burst wipes out eight consecutive bits in the scrambled sequence *(above)*. The receiving computer untangles the bits by again loading them horizontally into register rows and reading them out in vertical columns. The eight erroneous bits thus become distributed equally among the eight reassembled bytes *(below)*, where they can easily be handled by any of the detecting or correcting codes geared for lone errors.

01100101 00111001 01101111

Bytes of Light

In the early days of computing, the text printed on this page would have occupied more than thirty-five of the punched cards used to store data. Spread out on a tabletop, the punched cards would have covered an area of approximately six square feet. A storage medium that required more space for the copy than for the original was of small convenience, so computer designers steadily made improvements. In 1956, the first commercially available magnetic hard disk could condense these sentences into a space measuring just twelve square inches, a seventy-two-fold reduction.

Since the 1970s, a new kind of computer-storage device has emerged that can compress data into exquisitely small spaces. It uses the power and precision of a laser to etch and then read tiny marks on shimmering platters called optical disks. Already, optical disks have begun to rival or replace magnetic storage in some applications, and ultimately they may supplant microfilm or paper storage altogether. Such predictions are inspired by the medium's fantastic capacity: On an optical disk, the text on this page would occupy an area smaller than the period at the end of this sentence.

Optical disks offer several advantages besides greater data density. Because they store information so compactly, they are less expensive, bit for bit, than magnetic disks and tapes. They are also extremely durable. Some types of optical disks are expected to last many decades, whereas magnetic media often begin to deteriorate after a few years' use. Nor is there any chance of a catastrophic "head crash" occurring with an optical disk: Unlike the heads that read and write information on rigid magnetic disks, the lenses that focus the laser beam on the optical disk stand well clear of the surface.

Though still in its infancy, optical storage is evolving rapidly. The first generation of optical disks holds prerecorded information—moving video segments, music, data bases—that, like the contents of a book, cannot be altered or added to. The second generation of disks might be likened to pen and paper. Information can be written on the disk but not erased. For out-of-date information to be ignored, it must be cordoned off with markers that signal "old data—disregard." Following on the heels of the second generation is a third one bringing fully erasable optical disks, reusable millions of times. At the same time, inventors and engineers are working to adapt optical-storage techniques to other formats, among them plastic rectangles the size of credit cards and reels or cartridges of tape.

VISIONARIES OF THE VIDEODISK

Optical storage has a colorful past that began not with computers, but with television. In the 1920s, a Scotsman named John Logie Baird faced a problem. He had invented a device called the Televisor, a precursor of the television, and had sold a number of the machines to electronics enthusiasts in and around London. Once every day or so, the Baird Television Company broadcast a five-minute program to Televisor owners. In order for a Televisor to make sense of Baird's transmissions, however, a viewer had to adjust a scanner located inside the device so that it rotated at precisely the same speed as a similar device in the broadcasting studio. Achieving this synchronization consumed precious minutes: Indeed, by the time the Televisor displayed an intelligible picture, the broadcast might well have concluded.

In true inventor's fashion, Baird solved the problem with another invention. On conventional wax phonograph records, Baird pressed television signals representing a number of low-resolution still images. A special record player could then feed the signals into a Televisor while the viewer adjusted the set. Baird's recordings were the first use of disks to carry a video signal rather than an audio one. The Televisor was ahead of its time, and not until the late 1950s did researchers again attempt to capture video signals on disks. Among those reexploring the concept was an engineer by the name of David Paul Gregg.

Gregg had helped develop the first stereo phonograph records and early videotape machines for the television industry, and now he began to speculate about how the two technologies might dovetail. He approached a division of the 3M Corporation that had been spearheading the company's video research and offered his services as a consultant if 3M would underwrite a videodisk research project. The Minnesota tape manufacturer signed Gregg on and then enlisted an independent research and development organization called the Stanford Research Institute (SRI) to pursue the idea.

The SRI researchers eventually succeeded in producing a disk that could store several minutes of black-and-white video images, and became the first to record and view a television sequence from an optical disk. But research to incorporate sound and color halted abruptly in 1963, when 3M decided to cut off funding for the project.

Gregg remained undaunted. He dissolved his ties with 3M and set up his own company to continue refining videodisks. To bankroll the enterprise, Gregg drew on his earlier expertise in tape technology, developing a machine that could duplicate audio tapes at high speed. Although Gregg managed to sell a number of the machines to Philips, the Dutch electronics firm that was then pioneering the cassette tape, the proceeds failed to keep his videodisk company afloat. In 1967, Gregg sold out to the American entertainment conglomerate MCA.

Gregg's keenest interest had been to reproduce pictures, but he knew that videodisks could just as easily store information for computers. In 1964, he wrote: "The compactness of so much data on one reasonably flat, small area provides remarkably fast random access to any point on the disk. Almost a billion bits, instantly available and reliably reproduced, permit greater computer capacity and more efficient, faster use." It was a prescient statement, accurate even in its estimate of how much data a disk could hold. Still, it would take nearly two decades—and a grand flirtation with the videodisk as a picture medium—before Gregg's vision became reality.

A LIGHT APPROACH
Among the earliest suitors were Philips and MCA, who pursued the development of videodisk systems for the consumer. Videotape machines, the only other invention that was capable of delivering such goods, remained bulky and ex-

pensive devices in the 1960s, and most tape experts saw little hope of making them significantly smaller or less expensive. Philips and MCA therefore embraced the videodisk as a medium appropriate for home entertainment—a way of bringing movies and special programs into people's homes. In pursuit of that market, the two companies unveiled prototype players in late 1972. Much of the work that was subsequently done on optical-storage devices would draw heavily on their efforts.

At the center of the systems introduced by Philips and MCA is a laser *(pages 109-121)*, which emits a narrow beam of light that is focused on the underside of a spinning disk. Examination of this surface under a powerful microscope would reveal a tightly wound spiral of long, narrow bumps separated by flat intervals called lands. From the top, the bumps appear as pits and are usually referred to as such.

Extending for a distance of more than twenty miles, the spiral bears an average of twenty-six billion pits. The laser beam, which is focused to a point only one micrometer (one millionth of a meter) in diameter, follows the spiral from near the center of the disk to the disk's edge. When the laser beam hits a land, most of the light retraces its original path through the focusing lens; when the beam hits a pit, however, the light is scattered in such a way that most of it misses the lens. Whatever reflected light the lens does capture passes through additional lenses into a device called a photodetector, where the sequence of bright and dim flashes produces an alternating electrical signal that is converted into a color video signal. Although the alternating pits and lands give the videodisk a digital appearance, it is actually an analog medium: The variations in the length of the pits correspond to the continuously varying voltages that represent the video signal.

CORPORATE COMPETITION
Philips and MCA vied with each other for two years to produce consumer versions of the videodisk. But in 1974, the two agreed to pool their resources against competing videodisk formats announced by RCA and the Japanese electronics firm Matsushita.

Despite their head start, Philips and MCA took six years to bring their videodisk player to the commercial market. Even then the system continued to be plagued with problems, the thorniest of which arose in disk manufacture. To produce an optical disk, a laser beam records the spiral of information on a photosensitive surface, which covers a glass master disk. After processing, this master disk is used to produce one or more stamper disks. A clear plastic—the same material that contact lenses are made of—is molded onto the stamper, and a reflective coating of aluminum is deposited over the plastic. A final layer of plastic serves to protect the top of the metal. The resulting plastic-metal-plastic sandwich constitutes the videodisk itself.

Because stamper disks have limited lifetimes—some are good for only 1,000 pressings or so—a long manufacturing run of a videodisk can require many stampers. An exceptionally long run may demand that the maker prepare multiple master disks in order to turn out the necessary number of stampers.

Most of these manufacturing steps occur in "clean rooms"—areas kept scrupulously devoid of dust—for the slightest speck on the surface of a disk can obscure enough pits to produce visible interruptions, called "dropouts," in the television image. Making a perfect disk is an exacting process, and mastery of the skill eluded many early manufacturers. Indeed, flaws in a number of the first videodisks released to the public—including some produced by Philips and MCA—prevented them from playing as intended.

Philips's and MCA's competitors, in the meantime, fared no better. RCA took until 1981 to release its videodisk, and even then the advertising onslaught that heralded the system's arrival was not enough to conceal its shortcomings. Unlike the laser-based systems, the RCA system was built around a stylus that rode in a groove, as a phonograph needle does. The contact between stylus and groove would eventually wear out an RCA disk—which, like a phonograph record, was easily damaged. (The laser-based videodisk could in principle last indefinitely.) Furthermore, the absence of a laser in the RCA system made it difficult or impractical to include such features as freeze frame, slow motion, and reverse action. Viewers had little choice but to watch a program all the way through from start to finish.

Differences aside,the laser and stylus formats were both in trouble. By the late 1970s, several Japanese companies had built small, affordable videocassette machines that could not only play movies but also record them. Cable and satellite television proliferated as well, further invading the movie-market niche that videodisks had been expected to fill.

As a result, in the early 1980s Philips and MCA temporarily suspended their sales of consumer videodisk players. Matsushita likewise deferred the release of its system, quietly shifting its attention to recordable optical disks. RCA held out the longest; not until 1984 would the company finally abandon the quest that had cost it $580 million.

Ironically, within just a few years, the growth of a "gourmet video" market—made up of both American and Japanese customers seeking a medium that offered better picture and sound quality than those of videocassettes—would see the consumer videodisk reborn.

THE VIDEODISK RESURGENT

The videodisk is in essence a direct-access storage device. Little wonder, then, that the key to its resurgence—not only in the consumer market, but in commercial and industrial applications as well—was the computer. Each of the 54,000 circuits of the microscopic spiral on a standard videodisk produces a single video image; these images appear one after another at the rate of thirty per second when the disk is played, giving the impression of continuous motion. But since the laser beam of a videodisk player does not ride in a groove as a stylus does, it can skip back to the beginning of a particular revolution of the spiral over and over, holding a single image motionless on the screen. It is this faculty that grants random access, for a computer connected to a modern videodisk player can call up any of the 54,000 images in a few seconds or less. Depending on the viewer's responses to questions or choices that are programmed to appear on the screen, the computer software can also dictate which of the stored images will be displayed next.

Among the first to exploit that potential was M.I.T.'s Architecture Machine Group, established in 1967 to explore the benefits of combining technology and the arts. The group's most celebrated effort was a unique television tour of Aspen, Colorado, completed in 1980. When a viewer pressed a symbol on a touch-sensitive screen, images began to appear that transported the participant along an Aspen street. At each intersection, the viewer could turn left or right by pressing arrows on the screen. Meanwhile, a sinuous green line at the top of the screen charted the viewer's route.

The heart of the M.I.T. group's elaborate toy was a pair of videodisk players connected to a computer. Each videodisk contained 54,000 images of Aspen; through the use of vehicle-mounted, gyroscopically stabilized cameras pointing in four directions, all of the town's streets had been photographed at 10-foot intervals. As one videodisk displayed movement along one street, the other videodisk cued up the views possible along the next intersecting street. If the TV tourist chose to turn left or right, the second disk took over and the first moved ahead to the next intersection. These feats would have remained unaccomplished without the aid of a computer. Said M.I.T. professor Andrew Lippman, the director of the Aspen project: "You need an intermediary between you and that vast amount of pictorial data."

Myriad other forms of computer-videodisk synergy have evolved since the Aspen project. Kiosks where shoppers can order merchandise from catalogs on videodisk are quite common in hotel lobbies and airport terminals, and many American automobile manufacturers have developed videodisk training programs for their mechanics and dealers. And in a videodisk system that is designed to train medical students, the viewers respond to enactments of emergency-room situations—and pay the imaginary consequences that result from incorrect measures. "My patient died three times before I learned to save him," admitted one of the aspiring physicians.

THE DISK GOES DIGITAL

Despite Philips's disappointing start in marketing videodisks for the home-entertainment market, the company in 1980 signed on for a joint venture with Sony to create an optical disk in a new format. The two partners named their latest product the compact disk—CD for short. Originally conceived as a means of enhancing the living-room reproduction of recorded music, the twelve-centimeter (4.72-inch) compact disk was capable of holding more than one hour of noise-free, dynamically vivid music. The maximum playing length was set at seventy-four minutes—the amount of time needed to render an uninterrupted performance of Beethoven's Ninth Symphony.

Consumers were quick to embrace the new medium. Within just a few years, demand for compact disks had far outstripped supply, and stores selling nothing but CDs soon opened their doors.

The success of the compact disk hinges on its use of digital technology. To make a CD, an analog signal, representing the sound of music as a continuously varying voltage, is converted into its digital equivalent—a string of bits. These bits are then encoded as a pattern of almost two billion pits in a three-mile-long spiral. During playback, integrated circuits inside the CD player—in essence, a special-purpose computer—translate the pits and lands into bits and then re-convert the bits into music.

It became clear early on that compact-disk technology would lend itself to a broad range of computer applications, because the digital information that can be embossed on a CD is not restricted to music. The pits can equally well represent text, still pictures, or the moving images of video—anything that can be given digital form.

In 1984, Philips and Sony announced that they were working on a disk tailored for general-purpose data storage, primarily with desktop computers, rather than for the reproduction of music. The disk was dubbed CD-ROM, for Compact Disk-Read Only Memory. The "ROM" part of the label derives from the read-only memory chips found in computers; such chips store programs and data in permanent form and cannot be written over. In like fashion, a CD-ROM cannot accept new data; the disk merely delivers up whatever information the manufacturer has recorded on it.

The rigidity of that format is amply offset by the disk's capacity—more than 550 megabytes of data. A CD-ROM can thus hold hundreds of times more information than a floppy disk does. If the words on this page were to be encoded in digital form, for example, a CD-ROM could accommodate 250,000 pages just like it—and any of those pages could be summoned to a computer screen in a matter of seconds.

The first general-interest CD-ROM product was *Grolier's Electronic Encyclopedia,* released in 1985. The disk included only the text of the print original; the encyclopedia's nine million words occupied just twelve percent of the space available on the disk. Part of the unoccupied area was given over to an index of the encyclopedia that was half as long as the text itself. With its power to home in instantly on any key word or phrase occurring in the twenty-one-volume set, such an index makes the contents of the electronic encyclopedia more quickly accessible than those of its printed equivalent.

A number of other reference materials have appeared on CD-ROM: There are financial as well as educational data bases, even the entire white pages of all Canada's telephone directories. One CD-ROM brings together ten popular reference works on a single disk; these include *Bartlett's Familiar Quotations, Roget's Thesaurus, The World Almanac,* and the *U.S. ZIP Code Directory.* Yet even that compendium fails to fill the disk to capacity, a shortfall that conjures up the unimaginable in the world of computer storage: too much disk space and not enough data.

A RECONCILIATORY COUNCIL

In contrast with its audio cousin, CD-ROM has been slow to attract a following. Although CD-ROM drives are similar to audio-CD players, a CD-ROM machine requires additional decoding electronics to correctly interpret and display the data that a read-only compact disk contains. And unlike audio CDs, which were fully standardized before their public release, the first round of CD-ROM issues spoke a multitude of tongues: Each publisher used different indexing and retrieval schemes to arrange the information on disk, with the result that no disk worked with every player.

In a collective effort to impose order on the chaos, representatives from more than a dozen computer and electronics companies gathered in Stateline, Nevada, in 1985. The standard they settled on, named the High Sierra format after the hotel where the group held its meeting, proposed to codify the arrangement of data and directories on CD-ROM disks, organizing information in a format that any computer and any CD-ROM drive could be programmed to read.

Because the High Sierra format provides a uniform—and logical—method of filing digital data on CD-ROM, it was soon adopted, with slight modifications, by both national and international standards-setting organizations. That approval constituted one small step toward reconciling the incompatibilities between players and disks that had prevented CD-ROM from gaining broader acceptance.

The next step was to revise microcomputer control software, known as operating systems, so that the machines could read any optical disk that conformed to the High Sierra format. In early 1988, software and compact-disk publisher Microsoft led the way by making such modifications to their own operating system MS-DOS, which manages the flow of instructions and data in millions of IBM and other personal computers. Similar revisions to Apple Macintosh software soon followed.

While High Sierra remains the standard for CD-ROM computer data storage, more specialized formats continue to emerge. Philips and Sony, the developers of CD-ROM, champion one called Compact Disk–Interactive (CD-I). Intended for use with computerized players attached to television sets, CD-I would permit a viewer to browse through a disk storing text, graphics, animation, even sound. Digital Video Interactive (DVI), a rival system for use with microcomputers, would provide comparable features without the need for a special player.

Since the advent of CD-I and DVI, still more variations on the compact disk have been demonstrated, compounding the difficulty of predicting which CD formats will ultimately predominate. Perhaps the only certainty is that the compact disk will be increasingly called upon to carry all manner of digitized material into homes and businesses of all kinds.

THE SECOND GENERATION

Like magazines and books, CD-ROM and its variants are best suited to the publishing business. In order for their use to expand, however, optical disks must be made capable of accepting new information, as their magnetic cousins do.

Such disks actually predated CD-ROM. Relatively expensive and slow, they originally appealed to a limited audience only. They are designed to be written on only once, after which they can be read repeatedly. From that trait has sprung the technology's inelegant title: WORM (for Write Once, Read Many).

WORM disks consist of a layer of hard, clear plastic or glass covered on each side with a layer of metal or other materials that a laser beam can mark. To record data, the beam shines through the plastic or glass shell and permanently alters the information-carrying layer in some way—by burning a hole, by changing the color, by raising bubbles in the surface. Afterward, a laser beam too weak to affect the surface reads the marks.

Data on write-once disks cannot be erased or revised. Updates to information on the disk are recorded on a virgin area of the disk, and the old version is marked as out of date. Because such information is rendered obsolete rather than destroyed, special computer commands can resurrect it, yielding a detailed—and indelible—chronicle of the data that has been added to the disk over time. This feature often proves to be an asset for companies that need to maintain a complete record of prior transactions.

A JUKEBOX BELOW THE STACKS

WORM disks have been enlisted to help alleviate one of the biggest storage overloads of all—that of the Library of Congress in Washington, D.C. Although the library does not contain every book that has ever been published, it does hold a good number of them. More than 88 million items are cataloged there, and one new item is added to that list every ten seconds. With shelf space at a premium and land for expansion all but unavailable at any price, the library in 1982 embarked on a project to shrink its volume of documents through the use of optical disks.

The library has captured some of its most fragile documents—the Wright brothers' scrapbooks, for example—on sets of 30 to 300 WORM disks stored in a kind of jukebox. When a library patron asks, by means of a special, desktop image-display terminal, to review a document, the jukebox plucks the proper disk from the stack, and within seconds a facsimile of the document appears on the terminal screen. Not only does the system broaden access to these national heirlooms and reduce their wear and tear, it also frees prized shelf space in the library that the actual paper documents would otherwise occupy. "More than one million pages can be stored in just fifteen square feet of real estate," said Basil Manns, the project's chief engineer.

Depending on the content of the particular piece, material is recorded on the optical disks in either of two formats. When the sense of the document is more important than its appearance on the page, only the text is saved, either by typing it into a data base or, in some cases, by using a device called an optical character reader, which accomplishes the same result without the services of a human keyboardist. In the second format, documents that have compelling illustrations and those with calligraphy or handwriting of special interest are scanned by a machine that turns the document into a computer graphic. The scanner works by recording the reflectivity of the page at millions of individual points; thus, it captures the subtlest curve of a signature and translates color into a palette of grays.

The computer-graphic method has drawbacks. For example, it possesses a huge appetite for storage space. Even after the application of sophisticated data-compression techniques, an 8½-by-11-inch page in some cases consumes as much as a megabyte on a disk—five hundred times the amount of space required by a page of type stored as text.

Unalterable data on WORM disks may be a boon to accounting firms and to the Library of Congress, but for other applications the boon becomes a handicap. A large data base with constantly changing contents, for example, would soon fill a WORM disk. For these and similar uses, researchers have devised fully erasable optical disks, the most promising of which combine features of both magnetic and optical storage.

Called magneto-optic disks *(pages 120-121)*, they resemble optical disks in that they consist of a metallic surface protected by clear plastic. However, for this method of storing and retrieving information, the entire metal surface is magnetized in one direction, and the laser beam, instead of melting holes in the metal, heats a microscopic spot to just below its melting point.

Under these conditions, a magnet nearby can reverse the direction of the metal's magnetic flux wherever the beam strikes the disk. The slightest cooling of the metal fixes the flux in its new orientation. Then when the disk is read by another, less powerful laser, the beam reflects differently from points that are magnetized in one direction than it does from points magnetized in the other, making it possible for the encoded digital information to be detected. Data can be erased from the disk by a process of reheating each point and restoring its original flux orientation.

Controversy ushered in another class of optically erasable substances. In the 1960s, Stanford Ovshinsky, a self-taught physicist in Troy, Michigan, began experimenting with what are known as amorphous semiconductor materials. When heated to a particular temperature and then allowed to cool rapidly, some of these materials change from their reflective, crystalline state, or phase, to a duller, amorphous phase, and they remain in this state after they are allowed to cool. When heated to—and momentarily held at—a slightly lower temperature, the materials return to their crystalline phase. Ovshinsky recognized quite early that such phase-change properties would lend themselves to the manufacture of erasable optical disks.

Ovshinsky made a trip to Japan in 1974; he hoped that he would be able to persuade Matsushita to buy his process. The company had been investigating erasable optical disks ever since it had become disenchanted with the consumer videodisk. Matsushita seemed uninterested, however, and Ovshinsky returned to the United States without having struck a deal. The inventor had no better luck wherever he turned. "I felt very lonely out there for many years," Ovshinsky recalled years afterward.

Then in 1983, Matsushita announced a fully erasable optical disk. To Ovshinky's consternation, Matsushita's disk was based on amorphous semiconductor materials. The inventor considered the resemblance between his idea and the new Japanese product to be more than coincidental. He sued Matsushita, likening the company's actions to technological piracy. Matsushita claimed to have developed the idea independently but, reluctant to endure a lengthy court battle, the company soon settled with Ovshinsky by purchasing a license to develop his technology.

THE CARD THAT REMEMBERS

Ovshinsky was not the only inventor who played a role in helping shape the course of optical storage. There was also Jerome Drexler, a Bell Labs veteran who had established his own company in 1968 to manufacture photomasks—intricate stencils that are used to etch patterns photographically on computer chips. During the mid-1970s, as Drexler was looking for ways to diversify his product line, his decade of experience with optical technology led him to consider optical disks.

As they do today, most of the recordable optical disks in existence at that time featured a recording surface made from a thin film of metal. Drexler came up with an alternative recording medium, which he christened Drexon, that was based on conventional silver halide photographic emulsions—materials similar to those used in the manufacture of commercial movie film. Drexler and his assistant, Eric Bouldin, developed a chemical process that converted the relatively coarse grains of silver halide into a thin crust of extremely fine and highly reflective silver particles. A low-power laser then encoded data by burning microscopic pits, each of which represented a discrete bit of information, in this reflective crust.

Hoping that the low cost of the photographic supplies necessary for making Drexon would enable him to compete with the manufacturers of metal-based recordable optical disks, Drexler began selling his disks to companies that were producing optical read/write devices. Upon discovering that the market for such disks remained years from reaching commercial scale, however—and conceding that his own products were not much superior to thin-film metal disks—Drexler abandoned the pursuit.

Yet Drexler's optical-disk venture would bear fruit of another kind. One day in 1980, as he observed optical disks being punched from a square mold of Drexon, it occurred to Drexler that the scraps left over from the process might be cut into strips and mounted on a portable piece of plastic roughly the size of a credit card. Finding a way to read the information encoded on such a card would be a challenge, however, because the plastic rectangle could not be spun like a disk. Drexler got over that hurdle by arranging the data on the card in tracks spaced so far apart—five to ten micrometers—that a light beam could locate and read individual tracks as the card moved laterally through an inexpensive scanning device. The scanner relied on the simple reference of the card's straight plastic edge to guide the data tracks into position over the light beam; any tighter packing of information onto the card would have required the addition of sophisticated—and costly—servomechanisms, or tracking devices, to help the laser beam pinpoint information.

Drexler's optical-memory card was capable of storing up to two megabytes of information, with the data being registered in one of two ways: Either it could be photographically recorded in the Drexon during manufacture, or it could be added by a laser at any time thereafter.

Because Drexler anticipated that his profits would be generated by the sale of the cards themselves, his initial marketing scheme made no provision for the manufacture of the machines (called drives) needed to write on and read the cards. Instead, Drexler planned to license the drive technology to other companies and then manufacture as many cards as were needed for whatever applications those firms developed.

Although it was sound in theory, Drexler's strategy initially failed to pay off. No matter how promising a storage medium the optical-memory card was, it proved difficult to sell in a marketplace where few drives existed to render its contents intelligible. In response, the adaptable Drexler hired the Stanford Research Institute in 1981 to design a basic reader for the memory cards, and then he included that rudimentary hardware technology as an additional element of his licensing package.

To Drexler, the promise of the card appeared almost limitless. Company brochures spoke optimistically of applications in banking, retail businesses, and building security. Close to the top of the roster was medicine: A single card would be able to hold not only an individual's entire medical history—including such things as digitized X-rays, sonograms, or electrocardiograms—but also a record of that person's insurance coverage and a digitized photograph or signature that could be used to authorize treatment and prevent fraudulent misuse. Instantly accessible by a computer connected to a card-reading device, the medical details might come in handy should the cardholder ever be in an accident or require emergency hospitalization for some other reason.

By the mid-1980s, Drexler Technology had granted twenty licenses. To bring the optical-memory card squarely into the public view, however, would require the combined efforts of a brash quartet of college-age entrepreneurs.

A GREEN CARTEL

A Baltimore high-school student by the name of Douglas Becker had read about Drexler's cards in a computer magazine in 1983. Already young Becker was a confirmed technophile, having put together the hardware and software for a computerized shopping center. When he mentioned the card to Christopher Hoehn-Saric, his supervisor at the computer store where he was working at a part-time job, the two agreed that the card had potential. The pair got in touch with the businessman of the Becker family, Doug's older brother, Eric, who was holding down two part-time jobs while studying economics. Eric Becker in turn enlisted the aid of a stockbroker friend named Steve Taslitz. At the age of twenty-six, Taslitz was the oldest of the group, and he was the only one who held a college degree.

The foursome soon recognized that medicine was one of the card's more practical applications. Through the good offices of a physician friend who had a practice in Baltimore, they managed to get an appointment to have a meeting with a senior vice president of Blue Cross/Blue Shield of Maryland in January of 1984. The vice president was so taken with the idea of an optical-memory card that he invited them to present their concept to a group of forty top Blue Cross/Blue Shield decision makers. The quartet hurriedly sat down together to compose a business plan. "We did everything we could to make it look important," Taslitz remembered afterward. "We even bought a rubber stamp and marked 'CONFIDENTIAL' on each copy."

The presentation was a success. By October 1984, the group had signed a contract with Blue Cross/Blue Shield of Maryland, in which the insurer proposed to adopt the memory cards—now called LifeCards—for use by its 1.6 million subscribers. In return, the Becker group received $1 million over three years and royalties on the software systems developed for the cards. Drexler Technology benefitted as well, selling Blue Cross/Blue Shield of Maryland a license for $400,000 to market the cards.

Blue Cross/Blue Shield's campaign to introduce the LifeCard to its subscribers was somewhat rockier. The company announced the venture prematurely, touting the concept before the technology for manufacturing the card readers had been perfected. Then, in 1987, Blue Cross/Blue Shield stunned Drexler by signing a separate contract with the Optical Recording Corporation of Toronto, a rival optical-card firm. Still later, this contract, too, was allowed to lapse. Blue Cross/Blue Shield of Maryland had decided against optical cards for the time being.

The defection did little to deter other companies from pursuing optical-memory card applications of their own. In Japan, the Sumitomo Bank introduced Drexler's card as a substitute for money in the employee cafeteria, with workers buying a card for a certain sum and a card reader subtracting the correct amount from the records for every purchase they made.

Medicine, however, has remained the card's most promising use. To test the feasibility of issuing a card to every Italian citizen, Olivetti Corporation of Italy in 1988 purchased more than 20,000 cards to store the medical records of patients on the island of Sardinia. In another field trial, information-systems giant British Telecom tried out Drexler's cards at West London Hospital, cannily limiting participation in the program to maternity patients so that the card system could be evaluated in a single year.

FORMATS FOR THE FUTURE

Even though its potential remains to be fully realized, the optical-memory card is a reminder that disks are not the sole option in optical storage. Researchers are also working to refine optical tapes, which offer a much larger storage area than disks. As they do with magnetic computer tapes, users might have to spool through much of a reel to reach a desired section. But visionaries already foresee the day when optical tapes can hold a terabyte—that is, one million megabytes —of data on one reel.

Stacking several bits in a single spot—the goal of researchers working on an exotic technique called spectral-hole burning—offers a way to increase the capacities of optical storage media as much as a thousandfold. The technology capitalizes on the light-absorbing qualities of certain crystals. When a laser beam of a given frequency falls on such a crystal, groups of molecules inside the crystal absorb the beam's energy and become transparent to future laser beams of the same frequency. These transparent spots are known as spectral holes because only laser light of the established frequency will pass through them. Information is encoded digitally by allowing a hole to represent a one and the absence of a hole to represent a zero. By slightly changing the frequency of the laser light, another spectral hole can be created in the same spot as the first—and so on up and down the color spectrum. Researchers have established that as many as 1,000 spectral holes might be punched in an area no larger than the hole burned in a WORM disk.

Spectral-hole technology would permit 1,500 encyclopedia-size volumes to be lodged in an area the size of a fingernail, or all 88 million items in the Library of Congress to be stacked in a space no larger than a household refrigerator. The technique remains years from perfection, but in their ability to capture and release extraordinary amounts of information, spectral holes provide a vivid demonstration of just how far computer-storage technologies have come since the days of punched cards.

Preserving Data with Lasers

The optical-disk technology that produced CDs for the music industry promises a similar revolution for computers. Storage disks that, like CDs, yield up their contents by laser light are far more capacious than any magnetic storage medium. So precise is a laser beam that the smallest commercial version of these optical disks, just 4.72 inches in diameter, can hold 550 megabytes of information—several hundred times the typical storage capacity of a floppy disk of similar size.

Capacity is not the only advantage of optical disks. They are impervious to the heat, humidity, fingerprints, magnets, abrasion, wear, and even spilled coffee that can wipe out data on magnetic disks. They are also immune to head crashes (pages 62-63), so that backup copies to ensure the safety of essential information are not necessary. Their durability makes them useful for long-term data storage that would be impractical with magnetic methods.

Optical disks gain their permanence from the way they are made. For recording, a powerful laser makes a mark on a blank disk when signaled to do so, no mark when not signaled; it thus generates a pattern corresponding to the ones and zeros of binary code. For readout, a weaker laser scans the pattern. Reflections of the beam from the marks are detected by a photoelectric device. These are interpreted as digital data and are sent back to the computer.

The information-carrying pattern can be dots of dye or mineral, holes in metal, or pits in plastic. The pitted-plastic form has a special advantage for read-only disks, such as CD-ROMS: Such disks can be duplicated in a factory by methods similar to those used for phonograph records. Once a master is made with a laser beam, it can be used to produce a die that then stamps out copies in a press. By contrast, magnetic disks and tapes must be copied individually by re-recording, a more time-consuming and costly process.

Read-only videodisks and CD-ROMS were the first computer applications of optical disks, but newer types permit computer users to record data once and read many times or even to erase and re-record, working with optical disks just as they would with magnetic ones.

A Read-Only Optical Disk Drive

Although optical-disk drives vary in design, all of them include components like those in the read-only drive illustrated on these pages. A beam of light produced by a laser is directed through a series of lenses and other optical elements until it is focused on the surface of the spinning disk. The disk's pattern of reflectivity, which corresponds to the data it carries, bounces varying amounts of light back along its original path until the light reaches an element known as the beam splitter. There it is reflected through another series of lenses to a photodetector. At the same time, controlling servomechanisms keep the laser beam locked onto the desired part of the disk pattern by means of agile voice-coil motors (so named because they work on the same principle as the coils that drive a loudspeaker).

The drive reads from underneath while the disk spins above

the laser. However, when copies are stamped out in the factory, they are built from the bottom up: Pits are impressed on a clear plastic base; then a reflective layer of aluminum is added; and finally a lacquer coating is applied for protection. Because of this production method, the pits do not appear as depressions to the laser viewing the disk from underneath. Instead they appear as protrusions.

The tracks on optical disks can be followed with such accuracy by a beam of focused light that they can be packed densely to give immense storage capacities. Because of the limitations of its track-following system, a floppy disk may have only about a hundred tracks per inch; a hard magnetic disk may have several hundred. But a prerecorded optical disk has 16,000 tracks per inch, any one of which an optical-disk drive can pick out and read.

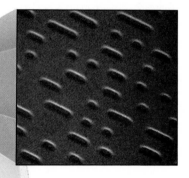

Topography of a disk. The pits on a prerecorded optical disk, here enlarged by a scanning electron microscope and seen from the laser's point of view, resemble parallel lines of regularly spaced ridges. Each of these protrusions—the underside of a recorded pit—is the size of a typical bacterium, about .6 micron (.6 millionth of a meter) wide. If 3,000 pits were lined up side by side, they would be about as wide as this letter o.

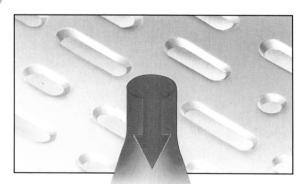

The land's bright spot. When the focused laser beam hits a flat space between pits—a so-called land—much of its light (red arrow) is reflected straight back toward the detector. At the point where the laser strikes the disk, it has been focused to a spot about a micron in diameter, almost twice as wide as a pit. This diameter is only a little larger than the wavelength of the laser light—the theoretical minimum. As a result, the beam, originally cone-shaped, assumes a cylindrical shape near its point of focus.

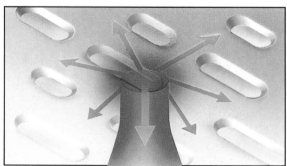

The pit's dark spot. When the focused laser beam hits the protrusion of a pit, much of the light is scattered sideways, so that very little is reflected back to the detector. Thus, each time the beam moves from a land to a pit, the reflected light changes in intensity, generating a detector signal that can be decoded to reproduce the recorded data.

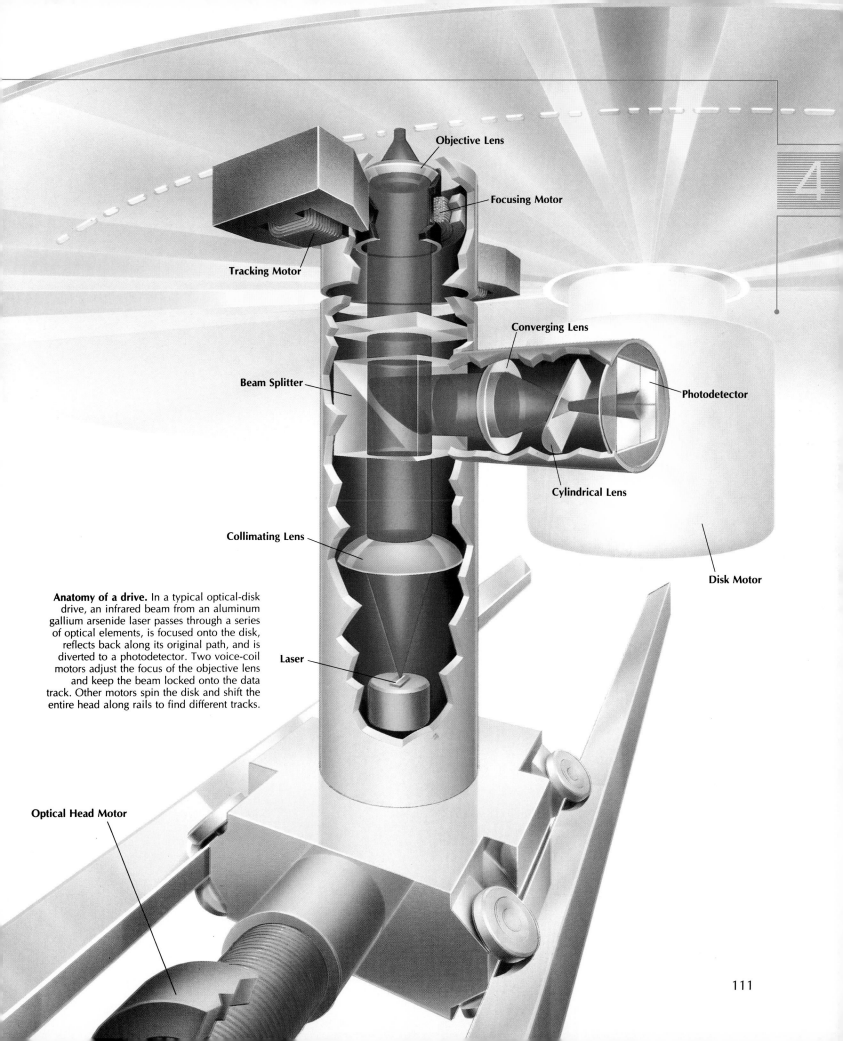

Objective Lens

Focusing Motor

Tracking Motor

Converging Lens

Beam Splitter

Photodetector

Cylindrical Lens

Collimating Lens

Disk Motor

Anatomy of a drive. In a typical optical-disk drive, an infrared beam from an aluminum gallium arsenide laser passes through a series of optical elements, is focused onto the disk, reflects back along its original path, and is diverted to a photodetector. Two voice-coil motors adjust the focus of the objective lens and keep the beam locked onto the data track. Other motors spin the disk and shift the entire head along rails to find different tracks.

Laser

Optical Head Motor

111

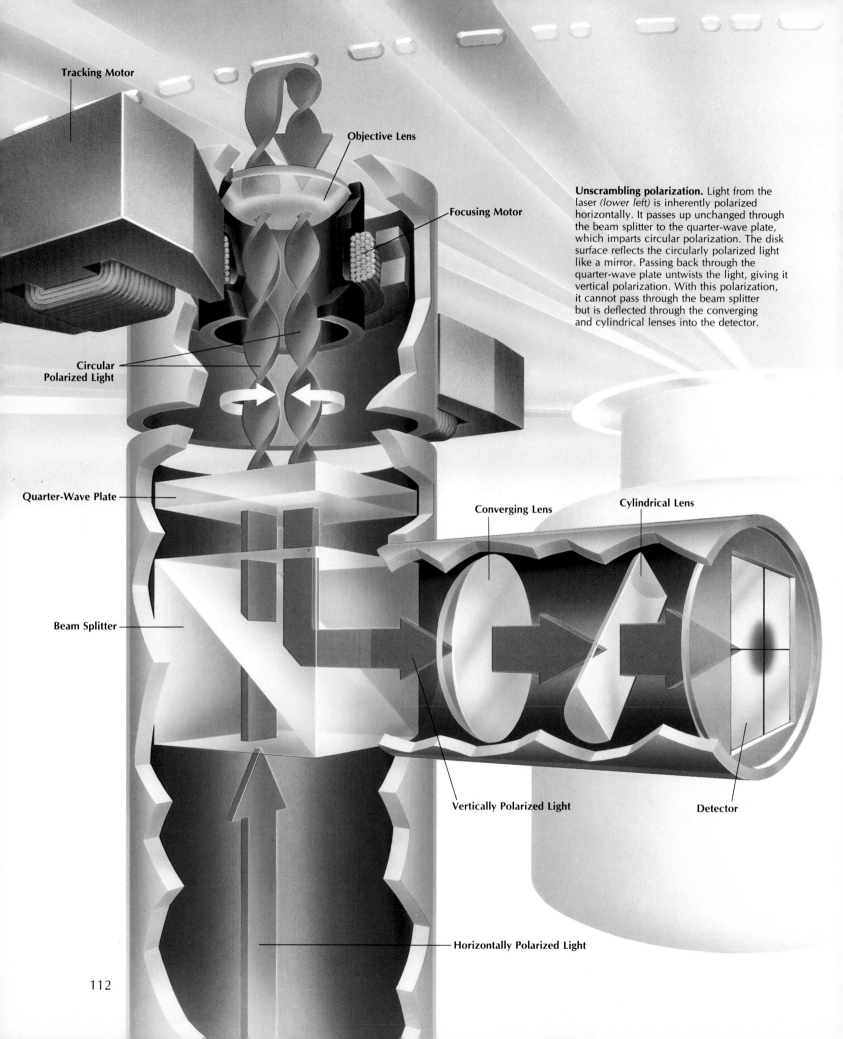

Tracking Motor

Objective Lens

Focusing Motor

Unscrambling polarization. Light from the laser *(lower left)* is inherently polarized horizontally. It passes up unchanged through the beam splitter to the quarter-wave plate, which imparts circular polarization. The disk surface reflects the circularly polarized light like a mirror. Passing back through the quarter-wave plate untwists the light, giving it vertical polarization. With this polarization, it cannot pass through the beam splitter but is deflected through the converging and cylindrical lenses into the detector.

Circular Polarized Light

Quarter-Wave Plate

Converging Lens

Cylindrical Lens

Beam Splitter

Vertically Polarized Light

Detector

Horizontally Polarized Light

112

Systems for Staying on Track and in Focus

The light waves generated by the laser in an optical-disk drive all vibrate in one direction—a phenomenon called polarization, which holds the key to controlling the beam and accurately reading the disk's contents.

Polarization of light can be likened to the baton that a drum major wields at the head of a marching band. When the drum major holds the baton vertically and moves it up and down as he marches forward, polarization is vertical. When he holds it horizontally and moves it from side to side as he marches, polarization is horizontal. If he spins the baton as he marches forward, polarization is circular—a corkscrew-like pattern of vibration.

To exploit these phenomena, the optical-disk system includes elements that reflect, transmit, or block different types of polarization. An element transmitting horizontal polariza-

tion but blocking vertical polarization, for example, might be likened to a rail fence. The fence would allow a drum major to pass his moving arm between rails so long as his arm went horizontally but would block it if it moved vertically. The beam splitter *(opposite)* does this, transmitting horizontally polarized light but reflecting vertically polarized light. A second element, the quarter-wave plate, slows a horizontally polarized wave so that it emerges with circular polarization or slows circular polarization to vertical polarization.

Working together, these elements send the laser beam up to the disk, then redirect the reflected light through lenses to the detector. The detector compares the amounts of light striking each of its four parts, in order to ensure that the laser stays focused on the disk and centered on the track that it is reading *(below)*.

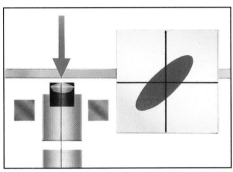

Lens too close. If the disk moves toward the lens, the light becomes a sharp, tilted oval. The northeast and southwest quadrants get more light, a signal for the focusing motor to move the lens back.

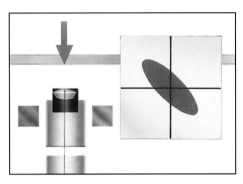

Lens too distant. If the disk moves away from the lens, the beam becomes a left-leaning oval, reversing the signal to the focusing motor and bringing the lens closer.

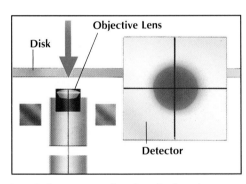

Lens in focus, on track. When the laser beam is properly focused on the center of the track *(red arrow)*, the reflected beam makes a fuzzy circle on the detector. Here, all quadrants of the detector receive the same amount of light, so no signal is sent to the voice-coil motors that guide the objective lens.

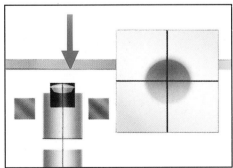

Beam inside track. If the track veers right, sending the beam inside the track, north quadrants of the detector receive more light because part of the beam falls only on lands. A correcting signal moves the lens right.

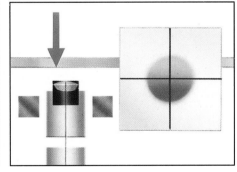

Beam outside track. Similarly, if the track veers to the left, the pattern of light on the detector is stronger to the south. A signal to the tracking motor returns the beam to the center before any data is misread.

Arranging Data on a Disk

All optical disks arrange their data in fine tracks that gleam with rainbow colors when seen by the naked eye, like the section in the background of this page. Two kinds of tracks are used. Most read-only disks have a single spiraling track, like a phonograph record (although it is read from the inside out rather than outside in). Other types of disk may use concentric circles, which are akin to those on magnetic disks (*page 48*) and offer faster access time.

In both kinds of track, data is divided into sectors, each sector containing equal amounts of information. On one sort of spiral-track disk, the sectors are also equal in length. But because they are moving in a circle, the outer sectors travel faster than the inner ones—a phenomenon familiar to anyone who has played crack-the-whip. To be read accurately, however, the sectors must all pass over the laser beam at the same speed. That means the disk drive has to change its rate of spin, turning the disk more slowly as sectors farther from the disk center are read. This need to vary spin rate to achieve a constant linear velocity (CLV) has a disadvantage: It makes the drive complex, and more important, it increases the time needed to find a given sector, because the disk must settle into a new rotational speed as the head moves in or out.

Other disk formats, including the concentric-track disk shown here, adjust for faster-moving outside sectors more simply. They stretch sector length while keeping spin rate steady—a constant angular velocity (CAV). Then, although some sectors travel faster than others, they all move past the laser beam in the same amount of time. For instance, if the land between two pits were 2 microns long at a radius of 3 inches, it would be 4 microns long at 6 inches to produce the same signal. This scheme simplifies the drive mechanism and lines up sector boundaries, speeding the search for sectors. But because some sectors are stretched out, it reduces storage capacity: A CAV disk can hold only about half as much data as a CLV disk of a similar size and track density.

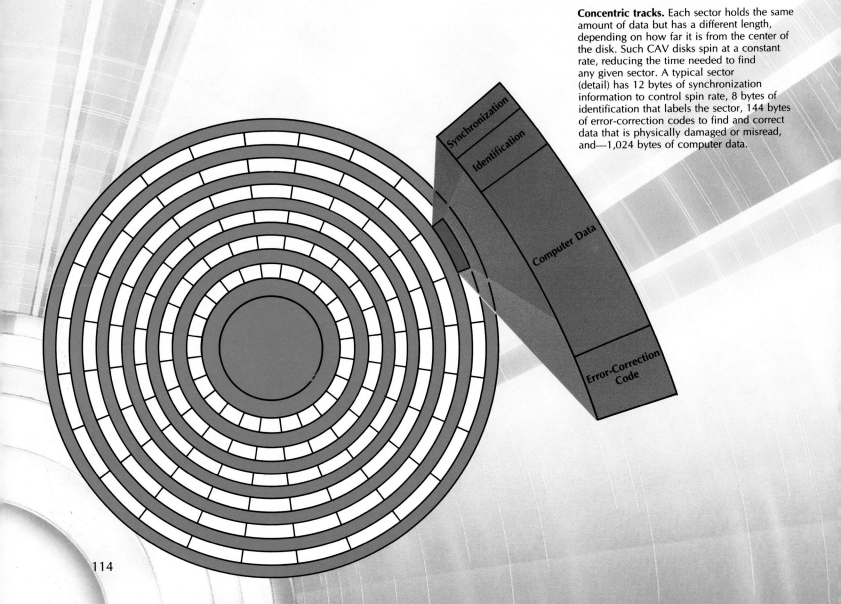

Concentric tracks. Each sector holds the same amount of data but has a different length, depending on how far it is from the center of the disk. Such CAV disks spin at a constant rate, reducing the time needed to find any given sector. A typical sector (detail) has 12 bytes of synchronization information to control spin rate, 8 bytes of identification that labels the sector, 144 bytes of error-correction codes to find and correct data that is physically damaged or misread, and—1,024 bytes of computer data.

Synchronization

Identification

Computer Data

Error-Correction Code

Two Kinds of Videodisks

All videodisks have spiral tracks, but one type uses CAV while a second employs the CLV method.

In a CAV videodisk, the track portion running once around the disk contains one sector corresponding to a single video frame. The sector is divided into two fields. One field contains data for half the lines in the image; the other provides the remaining lines, interlaced between the lines of the first field. Separating the fields are spaces for control signals.

Because a frame occupies one turn, it is easy to identify its beginning and end in order to hold, repeat, or skip a frame for special effects such as freeze-frame, slow motion, and fast search. But capacity is limited to a half hour of motion video per side.

The CLV videodisk fits more sectors into each turn as the spiral widens, doubling playing time. But beginnings and ends of frames are not easy to locate quickly, so special effects are more difficult to achieve.

Spiral tracks. This type of disk can have sectors of equal length *(right)* or of different lengths *(above)*. Sectors of the same length must be read at a constant linear velocity, meaning that the disk must spin at different rates, depending on which sector is being read. In the CD-ROM format shown here, each sector *(detail)* consists of 12 bytes of synchronization, 4 bytes of identification, 288 bytes of error-correction code, and 2,048 bytes of computer data.

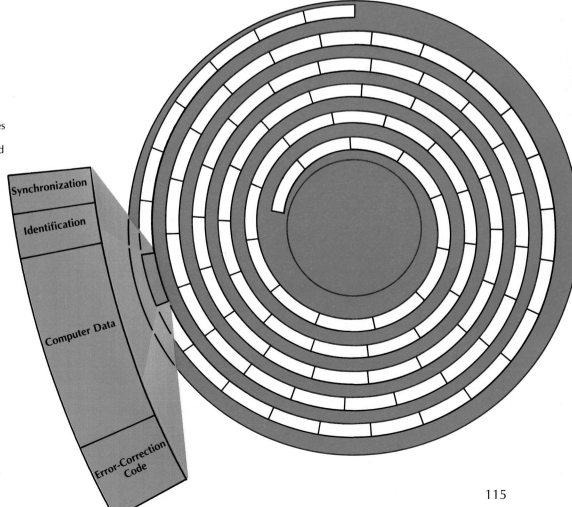

Synchronization

Identification

Computer Data

Error-Correction Code

Encoding Data: from Bits to Pits

In storing the binary digits of information on an optical disk, it may seem most logical simply to let a pit stand for a one and a land stand for a zero. But special coding methods cram in extra information by paradoxically requiring data to be expanded. Such codes generally replace data by symbols in which ones must have a specified number of zeros between them. The ones are physically represented not by pits but by transitions from pits to lands, while zeros are represented by the absence of such transitions.

CD-ROM disks use a code known as eight-to-fourteen modulation, in which each eight-bit byte is replaced by a fourteen-bit symbol having no fewer than two and no more than ten zeros between ones. There are 267 such fourteen-bit symbols, more than enough for the 256 possible combinations of ones and zeros in a byte. (The extra symbols are discarded.) For recording, special circuits use a lookup table (a kind of electronic dictionary) to convert each byte of data into its fourteen-bit equivalent, then insert "merge" bits after each symbol to ensure that the symbol ends do not violate the rules of the code. Merge bits also equalize the total lengths of pits and lands on a disk, helping drive controls to track data.

Many recordable optical disks use a different scheme, borrowing a code used for magnetic storage. It translates each byte into a sixteen-bit equivalent having no fewer than two and no more than seven zeros between ones.

These codes can cut the space needed to store data almost in half because they reduce the size of pits and lands. The laser reading beam is one micron wide; it overlaps and misses pits less wide. But by surrounding each pit with at least two lands, the beam can read pits only .6 micron wide.

A code from CD-ROMs. In the eight-to-fourteen modulation on CD-ROM disks, two bytes of data *(top row)* are replaced by fourteen-bit symbols *(middle row)* in which ones have at least two but no more than ten zeros between them. Groups of three merge bits then link successive fourteen-bit symbols into a steady stream *(lower row)* that follows the rules about maximum and minimum zeros. Each one in this bit stream thus corresponds to a transition from land to pit, as indicated by the square-wave binary signal used to create pits and lands on the disk *(bottom)*. Playback reverses the process.

11101000   11100010

00010010000010   10010001000010

010   00010010000010   000   10010001000010   001

Analog Recording for Video Images

In contrast to optical disks used to store digital data for computers, videodisks take an analog approach to storage: They store data in a continuously varying form analogous to the video signal being recorded. But the disks represent the analog signal with just two physical features: the transition from pit to land and the absence of a transition. The trick lies in the lengths of the pits and lands. They are not of specific sizes, their number corresponding to zeros and ones of digital data; instead, the pits and lands have variable size, their lengths corresponding to the values of the analog signal.

How this hybrid scheme works is indicated below in a diagram of the picture signal. (For simplicity, the sound portion is omitted.) The picture signal is a frequency-modulated, or FM, wave. The distance between successive peaks of the wave indicates information on image brightness, from black *(left)* through gray to white. The distance is measured by the time it takes the wave to cross and recross the baseline—125 nanoseconds for black, 109 for white—and this time determines the lengths of pits as indicated below the wave. Because the lengths of pits vary continuously, transitions to lands occur at varying times, allowing re-creation of the original signal.

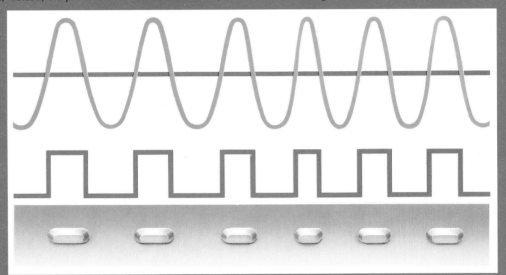

A code for recording. How the data at left would be translated into the so-called (2, 7) code used by some recordable disks is shown below. The two bytes *(top)* are converted into sixteen-bit symbols *(middle)* containing two to seven zeros between ones. To ensure these conditions at boundaries of symbols *(lower row)*, each byte has more than one seventeen-bit equivalent. Coding circuits choose an alternative with the proper number of zeros. As in the other scheme, ones in a coded signal determine pit-to-land transitions *(bottom)*.

11100010   10111010

100001000010010 0   010010000 1000100

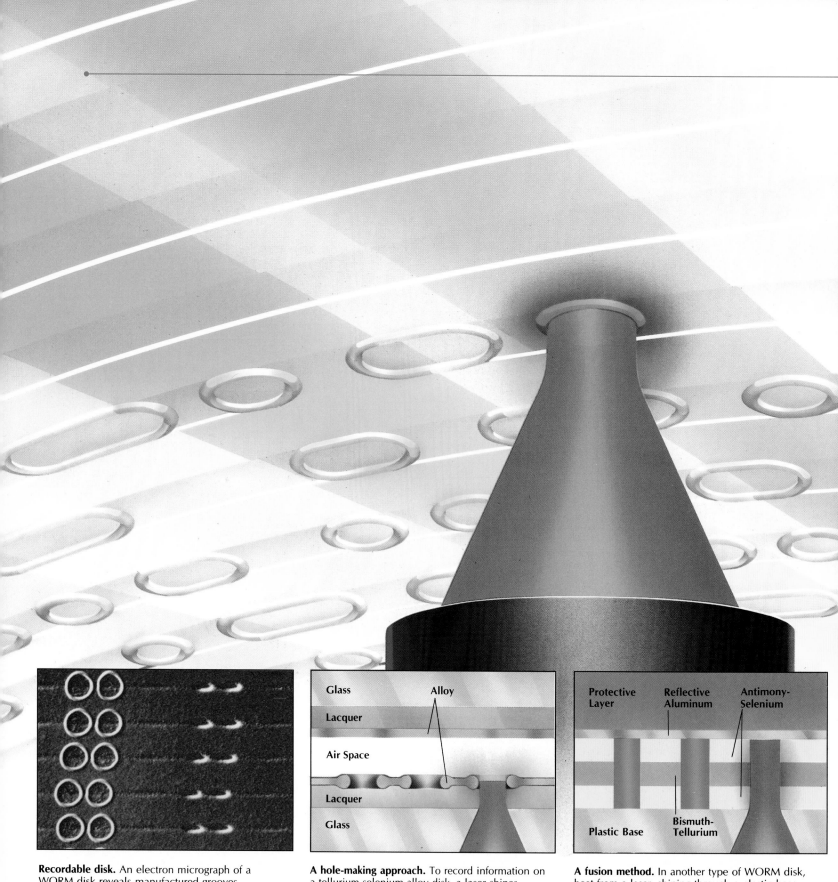

Recordable disk. An electron micrograph of a WORM disk reveals manufactured grooves that facilitate tracking, prerecorded pits *(above, left)* for synchronization and identification, and the holes of recorded data created by the heat of the high-power laser beam.

A hole-making approach. To record information on a tellurium-selenium alloy disk, a laser shines through the protective layers of glass to melt holes in the alloy; the air space accommodates the molten materials. When read, the holes are less reflective than their surroundings.

A fusion method. In another type of WORM disk, heat from a laser, shining through a plastic base, fuses two layers of antimony-selenium alloy with one of bismuth-tellurium alloy. A metallic plug forms that, during reading, is more transparent to laser light than is the surrounding unfused area.

Glass   Alloy
Lacquer
Air Space
Lacquer
Glass

Protective Layer   Reflective Aluminum   Antimony-Selenium
Plastic Base   Bismuth-Tellurium

Writing on Nonerasable Disks

Most of the optical disks that permit the user to record data can be written on just once, but thereafter this permanently recorded information can be read as often as desired. They are called WORMS—or write-once, read-many disks. To achieve the ability to record, WORMS need two special features: a disk material whose reflectivity can be permanently altered by a laser beam, generating marks that carry digital information; and a drive having a laser operating at two power levels, high for recording, low for reading.

Several types of recordable disk have been developed. The most common has one or more layers of metallic or organic materials that are easily melted by the high-power beam, creating a pattern of holes as indicated in the drawing at left. The holes differ from their unperforated surroundings on the disk, reflecting less—or in some systems, more—of the low-power reading beam. Other types of disks yield a similar pattern of marks when the beam forms bumps on the surface, creates pits in a layer of dye, or changes a crystalline metal to a less-reflective amorphous phase *(page 121)*.

WORM disks are ideal for storing information that need not and should not be altered, such as archives and images of documents. But because of their fantastic capacities—about a gigabyte (one billion bytes) on each side of a twelve-inch disk—they also can be used for data bases that need periodic revisions. When a file has to be updated, the corrected version is simply recorded in an unused part of the disk. The old file is then cordoned off with a marker, and another marker is inserted to tell where to find the new file on the disk.

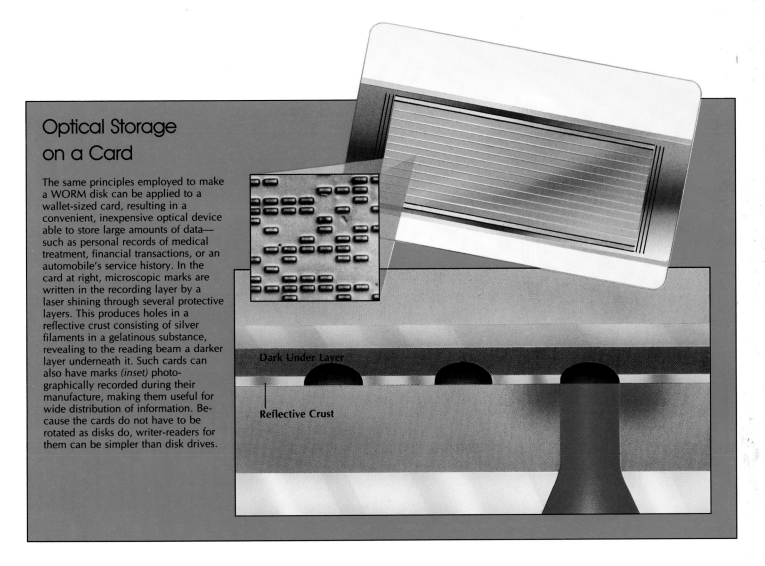

Optical Storage on a Card

The same principles employed to make a WORM disk can be applied to a wallet-sized card, resulting in a convenient, inexpensive optical device able to store large amounts of data—such as personal records of medical treatment, financial transactions, or an automobile's service history. In the card at right, microscopic marks are written in the recording layer by a laser shining through several protective layers. This produces holes in a reflective crust consisting of silver filaments in a gelatinous substance, revealing to the reading beam a darker layer underneath it. Such cards can also have marks *(inset)* photographically recorded during their manufacture, making them useful for wide distribution of information. Because the cards do not have to be rotated as disks do, writer-readers for them can be simpler than disk drives.

Dark Under Layer

Reflective Crust

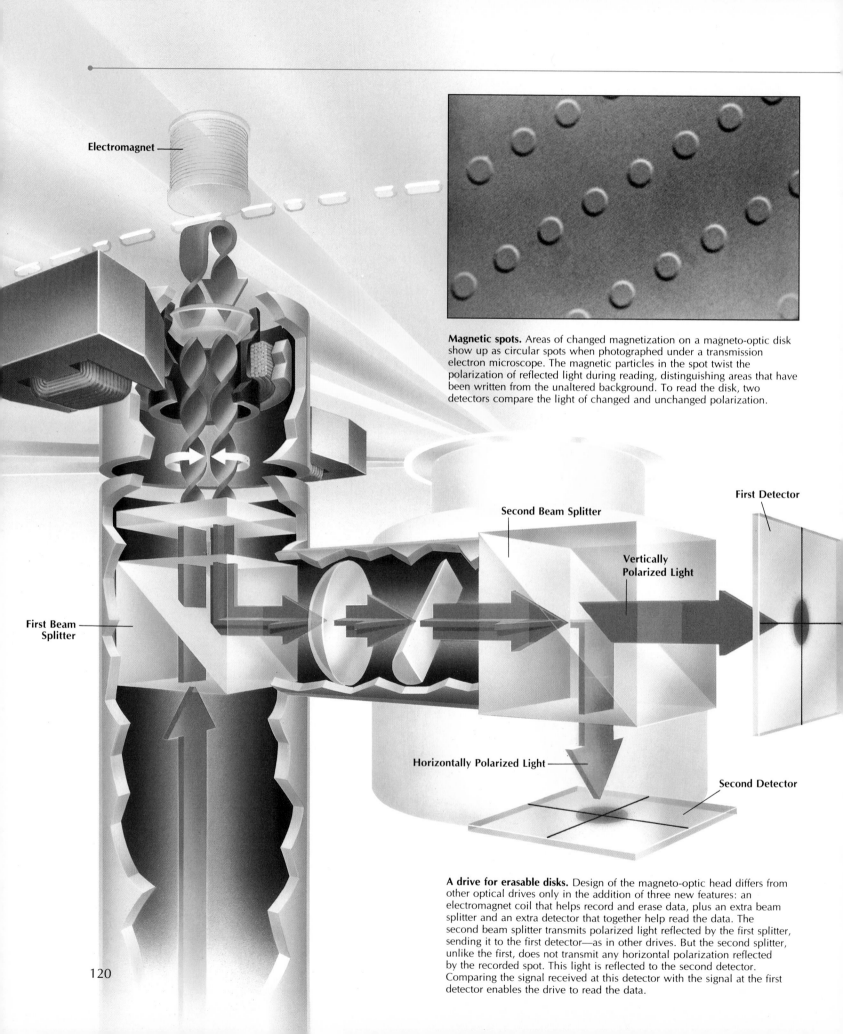

Electromagnet

Magnetic spots. Areas of changed magnetization on a magneto-optic disk show up as circular spots when photographed under a transmission electron microscope. The magnetic particles in the spot twist the polarization of reflected light during reading, distinguishing areas that have been written from the unaltered background. To read the disk, two detectors compare the light of changed and unchanged polarization.

Second Beam Splitter

First Detector

Vertically Polarized Light

First Beam Splitter

Horizontally Polarized Light

Second Detector

A drive for erasable disks. Design of the magneto-optic head differs from other optical drives only in the addition of three new features: an electromagnet coil that helps record and erase data, plus an extra beam splitter and an extra detector that together help read the data. The second beam splitter transmits polarized light reflected by the first splitter, sending it to the first detector—as in other drives. But the second splitter, unlike the first, does not transmit any horizontal polarization reflected by the recorded spot. This light is reflected to the second detector. Comparing the signal received at this detector with the signal at the first detector enables the drive to read the data.

Writing with Erasable Marks

To achieve the flexibility characteristic of magnetic disks, optical disks must permit the user not only to read and record data but also to change data that has been recorded previously. They need to be erasable.

One type of erasable disk uses both the magnetic and the optical properties of alloys of rare earth elements and iron or cobalt. These magneto-optic alloys have inherent magnetism, like ordinary bar magnets. At room temperature, they are highly resistant to any change in magnetization. But at a spot where a recording laser heats them, the inherent direction of magnetization can be reversed by an external magnetic field.

The change in the magnetization of the recorded spot causes it to slightly shift the polarization of a reflected beam, enabling the disk to be read by a special detector system. The spots of data are erased when they are reheated in the presence of a reversed magnetic field.

Another system, used for some WORM disks, depends on alterations in crystal structure. With so-called phase-change materials *(below)*, a laser switches certain metals between a highly reflective crystalline phase and a less reflective noncrystalline, or amorphous, phase. In yet another system, two lasers raise or flatten bumps in layers of dyes and plastics.

Electromagnet

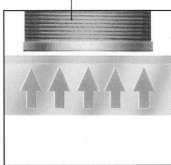 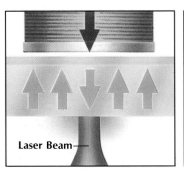  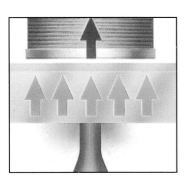

Laser Beam

The unrecorded disk. Before recording, particles *(orange arrows)* on a magneto-optic disk are all magnetized in the same direction *(up, here)*, at right angles to the surface of the disk.

Recording. To write on the disk, a coil is switched on, with its magnetic field *(purple arrow)* oriented opposite to the direction of magnetic particles on the unrecorded disk. Where the recording beam heats the disk, the magnetization of the particles is reversed by the external magnetic field.

Reading. With the external magnet switched off, a low-power beam reflects off the spot of reversed magnetization. Its reversed magnetization twists polarization of the beam relative to polarization of reflections from unrecorded areas, generating a signal to be read by the paired detectors.

Erasing. The original magnetic direction can be restored to the recorded spot by reheating with the electromagnet turned on so that its field *(purple arrow)* now matches the upward orientation of an unrecorded area, causing the magnetization of the particles at the spot to reverse.

Putting Erasable Data into Crystals

Under an electron microscope, the blank crystalline areas of a disk of selenium and tellurium compounds are brightly reflective. But in those areas where a short, intense laser pulse has melted the disk, the orderly pattern of molecules in a crystal is disrupted, creating a so-called amorphous phase, in which molecules are randomly oriented and less reflective—dark ovals representing data *(right)*. But these spots can also be returned to their bright crystalline state by reheating them and cooling them more gently—for instance, with an oval laser beam that is hot at its leading edge and cool at its trailing edge. Such disks are cheaper and generate a stronger signal than do magneto-optic disks. However, early versions have lacked the ability to undergo as many write-erase cycles as magneto-optic disks, a limit to their usefulness.

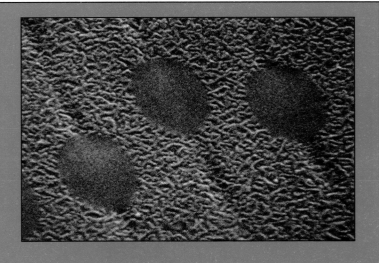

Glossary

Access time: the average time it takes a computer to find information in memory or to retrieve it from a storage device.

Acoustic delay line: an early form of computer memory consisting of a mercury-filled glass tube with quartz crystals at either end; the crystals convert electrical pulses representing data into vibrations that travel as sound waves through the mercury.

Address: the numbered location of a bit or word in a computer's memory.

Bit: the smallest unit of information processed or stored by a computer, represented by a single zero or one. The word "bit" is a contraction of "binary digit."

Bit cell: the magnetized area on a tape or disk that represents a single binary digit.

Byte: a series of eight bits treated as a unit for computation or storage.

Cathode-ray tube (CRT): a television-like display device with a screen that lights up where it is struck from the inside by a beam of electrons.

CD-ROM (compact disk read-only memory): a type of compact disk used to store text or graphics in digital form.

CD-I (compact disk-interactive): a CD-ROM format capable of storing audio, animated, textual, and graphics data; intended for use with a special player attached to a television set.

Cell: a single location in a computer's memory, capable of storing one bit of information.

Central processing unit (CPU): the part of a computer that interprets and executes instructions, as well as overseeing the transfer of data to and from both memory and storage; it is composed of a processor, a control unit, a clock, and a small amount of memory.

Checksum: an extra byte derived from a group of bytes and appended to them to enable a computer to detect errors after data has been transmitted or stored.

Chip: *See* Integrated circuit.

Clock: a device, usually based on a quartz crystal, whose regular pulses coordinate all computer operations.

Compact disk (CD): a storage device for audio or other data that permanently records information in digital form as a series of pits, or depressions, etched by laser into the surface.

Core memory: a type of computer memory that stores data on tiny magnetized rings suspended in a grid of current-carrying wires.

Data base: a collection of facts about a subject or subjects, divided into files and records that are organized for easy access.

Data-base management system: software that organizes and provides ready access to the information in a data base.

Data compression: a method for reducing the number of bits needed to store information.

Direct access: the ability to retrieve a specific piece of information directly from storage without having to search sequentially through data. *See also* Random-access memory; Serial access.

Disk: a round plate made of plastic, metal, or glass and used for storing data either magnetically or optically. *See also* Floppy disk; Hard disk; Optical disk.

Disk drive: a device that spins a magnetic or optical disk so that data can be stored on it or recovered from it.

Domain: a microscopic clump of magnetically aligned atoms in a substance such as iron that creates a magnetic field oriented in one direction.

DVI (Digital Video Interactive): A CD-ROM format similar to CD-I, but intended for use with a general-purpose microcomputer.

Electromechanical relay: a type of switch consisting of a coil of wire wrapped around a small iron bar; current through the wire magnetizes the bar and activates the switch.

Exclusive-OR function: one of a computer's basic logic operations, which yields a zero when combining two bits that are alike and a one when the bits are different.

Floppy disk: a flexible plastic platter with a magnetic coating on both sides, used for storing digital data; the disk is housed in a protective jacket and can easily be transported from one computer's disk drive to that of another.

Garbage collection: a software strategy that identifies unneeded data and removes it from memory to make room for new data.

Hamming codes: any of several error-correction techniques, based on logical relationships established between data and check bits, that enable a computer to pinpoint the location of an error in a group of bits and thus correct it.

Hard disk: a rigid metallic platter coated on both sides with a thin layer of magnetic material, where digital data is stored; hard disks have more storage capacity than floppy disks but are usually permanently installed in a computer's disk drive and thus are less portable.

Head crash: a catastrophic malfunction in a hard-disk drive that occurs when the read/write head touches the spinning disk, gouging its magnetic surface and destroying both data and the head.

Hierarchical data base: an organizational system resembling an inverted tree, with individual data-base records arranged into groups and subgroups.

Integrated circuit: an electronic circuit made up of thousands of transistors and other electronic components, all formed on a single piece of semiconductor material; also known as a chip.

Interleaving: the orderly shuffling together of bits from different computer words to protect against a string of adjacent errors; after transmission, when the words are reassembled, adjacent errors are separated and can be handled individually.

Land: a flat space between pits on the track of an optical disk; patterns of lands and pits are used to represent either analog or digital information.

Magnetic drum: a metallic cylinder on which electronic pulses representing data are stored magnetically.

Magnetic tape: plastic tape coated on one side with a magnetic material that stores information as varying patterns of magnetization.

Magneto-optic disk: an optical disk that combines principles of both magnetic and optical storage, permitting the erasure and rewriting of data.

Memory: the principal area within a computer for storing instructions and data, typically composed of integrated circuits capable of holding thousands or millions of bits apiece.

Multiprogramming: the ability in a computer to switch rapidly among several programs in memory to give the appearance that all are being run simultaneously.

Network data base: a system of data organization in which any discrete group of facts, or record, can be linked to any other.

Optical disk: a storage medium that holds information in the form of a pattern of marks on a rigid platter; an optical-disk drive reads, erases, or writes data on the disk with a laser beam.

Page: the result of dividing a program or data into portions of equal size, each stored as a unit in memory or on disk or tape.

Parity check: an error-detection method that appends either a one or a zero to a group of bits to make the total number of ones even; after transmission or storage, a change from even to odd indicates an error. Some parity-check systems establish an odd number of ones and watch for an even number as a sign of an error.

Purging: in a computer's memory, the automatic erasure of stale information to create more storage space.

Random-access memory (RAM): a form of temporary memory, the contents of which can be altered by the user; it provides direct, rather than serial, access to stored information.

Read/write head: the part of a tape drive or a disk drive that both retrieves data from a tape or disk and records data on it.

Record: the basic organizational unit of a data base, consisting of a group of facts about a particular subject.

Relational data base: a data base that does not require predetermined relationships among individual records but can uncover hidden connections or establish new ones at any time.

Sector: a wedge-shaped division on a disk that subdivides each track, facilitating access to specific pieces of data.

Segment: the result of dividing a program or data into portions of unequal size, the better to accommodate the spaces available in a computer's memory.

Serial access: a method of retrieval in which a computer must search sequentially through stored data to find a specific piece of information. *See also* Direct access.

Slider: the read/write head of a hard disk; it floats above the surface on a cushion of air.

Storage: devices such as disks and tapes that store data either magnetically or optically; though slower than a computer's internal electronic memory, storage devices provide virtually unlimited capacity and preserve data indefinitely.

Track: the narrow band on a disk or tape where data is stored. A disk track is either one revolution of a continuous spiral filling the whole disk or one of a series of concentric circles; tape tracks run the length of the tape.

Transistor: an electronic switching device that can amplify a voltage or turn a current on or off to represent either a zero or a one of binary data; the integrated circuits of a computer's memory contain thousands or millions of transistors apiece.

Vacuum column: the part of a tape-drive system that controls the slack in the supply and take-up reels.

Videodisk: an optical disk that stores analog video signals.

Virtual memory: a technique for handling programs too large to fit all at once into a computer's memory; programs and data are divided into pages or segments that are stored on disk or tape and loaded into memory only as needed for the program's execution. *See also* Page; Segment.

Williams tube: a computer-memory device that stores binary data as dots and dashes on a CRT screen.

Word: a group of bits, ranging from eight to sixty-four, treated as a unit by a computer and capable of being stored at a single memory address. *See also* Byte.

WORM (write once, read many) disk: an optical disk on which a user can write information; once the data is recorded, it can be read repeatedly but never changed or erased.

Bibliography

Books

Augarten, Stan, *Bit by Bit*. New York: Ticknor & Fields, 1984.

Bashe, Charles J., et al., *IBM's Early Computers*. Cambridge, Mass.: The MIT Press, 1986.

Bouwhuis, G., et al., *Principles of Optical Disc Systems*. Boston: Adam Hilger Ltd., 1985.

Camras, Marvin, *Magnetic Tape Recording*. New York: Van Nostrand Reinhold, 1985.

Curran, Susan, and Ray Curnow, *Overcoming Computer Illiteracy: A Friendly Introduction to Computers*. New York: Penguin Books, 1983.

Ditlea, Steve, ed., *Digital Deli*. New York: Workman Publishing, 1984.

Fisher, Franklin M., James W. McKie, and Richard B. Mancke, *IBM and the U.S. Data Processing Industry*. New York: Praeger Publishers, 1983.

Fishman, Katharine Davis, *The Computer Establishment*. New York: Harper & Row, 1981.

Gelatt, Roland, *The Fabulous Phonograph: From Edison to Stereo*. New York: Appleton-Century, 1966.

Giarratano, Joseph C., *Modern Computer Concepts*. Indianapolis, Ind.: Howard W. Sams & Co., 1982.

Gillenson, Mark L., *Database: Step-by-Step*. New York: John Wiley & Sons.

Hamming, Richard W., *Coding and Information Theory*. Englewood Cliffs, N. J.: Prentice Hall, 1986.

Hayes, John P., *Computer Architecture and Organization*. New York: McGraw-Hill, 1978.

Helms, Harry, ed., *The McGraw-Hill Computer Handbook*. New York: McGraw-Hill, 1983.

Hnatek, Eugene R., *A User's Handbook of Semiconductor Memories*. New York: John Wiley & Sons, 1977.

Johnson, George, *Machinery of the Mind*. New York: Times Books, 1986.

Kean, David W., *IBM San Jose: A Quarter Century of Innovation*. San Jose, Calif.: International Business Machines Corporation, 1977.

Lambert, Steve, and Suzanne Ropiequet, *CD ROM: The New Papyrus*. Redmond, Wash.: Microsoft Press, 1986.

Lambert, Steve, and Jane Sallis, eds., *CD-I and Interactive Videodisc Technology*. Indianapolis, Ind.: Howard W. Sams & Co., 1986.

Lavington, Simon H.:
A History of Manchester Computers. Manchester, England: National Computing Centre, 1975.
Early British Computers. Bedford, Mass.: Digital Press, 1980.

Lukoff, Herman, *From Dits to Bits: A Personal History of the Electronic Computer*. Portland, Ore.: Robotics Press, 1979.

McLeod, Jonah, *Winchester Disks in Microcomputer Systems*. 2nd ed. Oxford, England: Elsevier International Bulletins, 1986.

Matthewson, David K., *Revolutionary Technology*. Boston: Butterworth & Co., 1983.

Metropolis, N., J. Howlett, and Gian-Carlo Rota, eds., *A History of Computing in the Twentieth Century*. Orlando, Fla.: Academic Press, Inc., 1980.

Myers, Patti, *Publishing with CD-ROM*. Arlington, Va.: National Composition Association, 1986.

Peterson, W. Wesley, and E. J. Weldon, Jr., *Error-Correcting Codes*. Cambridge, Mass.: The MIT Press, 1972.

Pohm, A. V., and O. P. Agrawal, *High-Speed Memory Systems*. Reston, Va.: Reston Publishing, 1983.

Prince, Betty, and Gunnar Due-Gunderson, *Semiconductor Memories*. New York: John Wiley & Sons, 1983.

Pugh, Emerson W., *Memories That Shaped an Industry*. Cambridge, Mass.: The MIT Press, 1984.

Ralston, Anthony, and Edwin D. Reilly, Jr., eds., *Encyclopedia of Computer Science and Engineering*. New York: Van Nostrand Reinhold Company, 1983.

Redmond, Kent C., and Thomas M. Smith, *Project Whirlwind: The History of a Pioneer Computer*. Bedford, Mass.: Digital

Press, 1980.

Slotnick, Daniel, et al., *Computers and Applications*. Lexington, Mass.: D. C. Heath and Company, 1986.

Teja, Edward R., *The Designer's Guide to Disk Drives*. Reston, Va.: Reston Publishing, 1985.

Walsh, Myles E., *Database and Data Communications Systems*. Reston, Va.: Reston Publishing, 1983.

Wang, An, and Eugene Linden, *Lessons: An Autobiography*. Reading, Mass.: Addison-Wesley Publishing, 1986.

Wexelblat, Richard L., ed., *History of Programming Languages*. New York: Academic Press, 1981.

Wiederhold, Gio, *Database Design*. New York: McGraw Hill, 1983.

Williams, Michael R., *A History of Computing Technology*. Englewood Cliffs, N.J.: Prentice-Hall, 1985.

Periodicals

Amsterdam, Jonathan, "Data Compression with Huffman Coding." *BYTE*, May 1986.

"An Wang's Early Work in Core Memories." *Datamation*, Mar. 1976.

Badgett, Tom, "Hard Disk Drives for the Masses." *Computers and Electronics*, Apr. 1985.

Barney, Clifford, "Award for Achievement." *Electronics Week*, Jan. 14, 1985.

Bonn, Ted, "Developing Univac's Plated Thin Metal Recording Tape." *The Computer Museum Report*, Fall 1983.

Brede, D. W., "Magnetic Head Design Parameters Focus on Read-Write Processes." *Computer Technology Review*, Winter 1983.

Brewer, Bryan, "U.S.-Made CD-ROM Software: A Burst of Activity." *Digital Audio*, Mar. 1987.

Bush, Vannevar, "As We May Think." *The Atlantic Monthly*, July 1945.

Chaudhari, Praveen, "Electronic and Magnetic Materials." *Scientific American*, Oct. 1986.

Chi, Chao S., "Higher Densities for Disk Memories." *IEEE Spectrum*, Mar. 1981.

Cohen, Jacques, "Garbage Collection of Linked Data Structures." *Computing Surveys*, Sept. 1981.

Colwell, T. David, and Hubert Song, "Servos Keep 5¼-in. Winchesters on Track." *Mini-Micro Systems*, Feb. 1982.

"Conversation: Jay W. Forrester" (Christopher Evans, interviewer). *Annals of the History of Computing*, July 1983.

Denning, Peter J.:
"The Science of Computing: Virtual Memory." *American Scientist*, May/June 1986.
"Third Generation Computer Systems." *Computing Surveys*, Dec. 1971.
"Virtual Memory." *Computing Surveys*, Sept. 1970.

Evans, David C., "Computer Logic and Memory." *Scientific American*, Sept. 1966.

Fishman, Steve, "Their Fortune Was in the Cards." *Success!*, April 1986.

Fong, Kirby W., "The NMFECC Cray Time-Sharing System." *Software—Practice and Experience*, Jan. 1985.

Free, John, "The Laser-Disc Revolution." *Popular Science*, May 1985.

"From Mozart to Megabytes." *Time*, Mar. 16, 1987.

Golomb, Solomon W., "Optical Disk Error Correction." *BYTE*, May 1986.

Gordon, Jason H., "Choosing the Best Tape Drive." *Mini-Micro Systems*, Oct. 1982.

Hamilton, F. E., and E. C. Kubie, "The IBM Magnetic Drum Calculator Type 650." *Annals of the History of Computing*, Jan. 1986.

Hammar, Peter, and Don Ososke, "The Birth of the German Magnetophon Tape Recorder 1928-1945." *db*, Sept./Oct. 1985.

Hecht, Jeff, "Store It with Light." *Computers & Electronics*, July 1984.

"Here Comes the Erasable Laser Disk." *Fortune*, Mar. 4, 1985.

Hoagland, Albert S., "Information Storage Technology: A Look at the Future." *Computer*, July 1985.

Hoban, Phoebe, "Laser Cards: Artificial Intelligence." *OMNI*, Dec. 1983.

Howe, Dennis G., Harold T. Thomas, and Joseph J. Wrobel, "Replication of Very High-Density Video Disc Master Recordings via Contact Printing." *Photographic Science and Engineering*, Nov./Dec. 1979.

IBM Journal of Research and Development, Sept. 1981.

"In Search of the Laser Eraser." *The Economist*, July 13, 1985.

Jarvis, Stan, and Steve Booth, "A Century of Optical Disc Development" (series). *Videodisc News*, July-Nov. 1982.

Kenney, George C., "Special Report: A Time Line of Videodisc Milestones." *The Videodisc Monitor*, April 1985.

Krajewski, Rich, "Database Types." *BYTE*, Oct. 1984.

"Lights! Camera! Ketchup!" *Hippocrates*, May/June 1987.

McEliece, Robert J., "The Reliability of Computer Memories." *Scientific American*, Jan. 1985.

McLeod, Jonah, "Optical Disks Loom as Replacement for Tape." *Electronic Design*, Sept. 30, 1981.

McManus, Reed, "CD-ROM: The Little Leviathan." *PC World*, Vol. 4, Issue 10.

Manns, Basil, and Tamara Swora, "Books to Bits: Digital Imaging at the Library of Congress." *Journal of Information & Image Management*, Oct. 1986.

Martin, Gary, "Virtual Memory Management Expands Microprocessors." *Computer Design*, June 1983.

"Microsoft: Ushering in the CD-ROM Era." *High Technology*, Nov. 1986.

Mills, Mark, "Memory Cards: A New Concept in Personal Computing." *BYTE*, Jan. 1984.

Moad, Jeff, "Pinning Hopes on a Vision of Storage." *Datamation*, Feb. 1, 1987.

Moore, Steve, "The Mass Storage Squeeze." *Datamation*, Oct. 1984.

Ohr, Stephan, "Magneto-Optics Combines Erasability and High-Density Storage." *Electronic Design*, July 11, 1985.

Oliver, Ted A., "Embedded Servo Controllers Push up Disk Storage." *Mini-Micro Systems*, Dec. 1984.

Onosko, Timothy, "Let There Be Light." *Creative Computing*, Sept. 1985.

Pingry, Julie, ed., "Optical Disk Technology Creates a New Class of Peripheral." *Digital Design*, Aug. 1984.

Porter, Martin:
"Optical Storage." *Computers and Electronics*, April 1985.
"Ovshinsky: Optical Storage Pioneer." *Computers & Electronics*, July 1984.

Pournelle, Jerry, "CD-ROMs Are Facing a Limited Life Span." *InfoWorld*, Mar. 17, 1986.

Price, Joseph, "The Optical Disk Pilot Program at the Library of Congress." *Videodisc and Optical Disk*, Nov./Dec. 1984.

Rice, Philip, and Richard F. Dubbe, "Development of the First

Optical Videodisc." *SMPTE Journal,* Mar. 1982.

Richman, Barry, "Dense Media and the Future of Publishing." *Publishers Weekly,* Mar. 21, 1986.

Rosen, Saul, "Electronic Computers: A Historical Survey." *Computing Surveys,* Mar. 1969.

Rothchild, Edward S.:
"An Eye on Optical Disks." *Datamation,* Mar. 1, 1986.
"Optical Memory: Data Storage by Laser." *BYTE,* Oct. 1984.

Sandberg-Diment, Erik, "Squeezing Stored Data." *New York Times,* Feb. 24, 1987.

Sehr, Barbara K., "High Noon for CD-ROM." *Datamation,* Nov. 1, 1986.

Seither, Michael, "Old Problem, New Light." *Forbes,* Dec. 3, 1984.

Serrano, Clara I., "Virtual Memory: 'Mind Expander' for Microcomputers." *Machine Design,* Apr. 24, 1986.

Shiell, Jon, "Virtual Memory, Virtual Machines." *BYTE,* 1986 extra edition.

Shuford, Richard S., "CD-ROMs and Their Kin." *BYTE,* Nov. 1985.

Solomon, Les, and Stan Veit, "Data Storage in a Nutshell." *Computers & Electronics,* July 1983.

"Special Report: The Options Multiply in Mass Storage." *Electronics,* May 19, 1986.

Suits, J. C., et al., "Lorentz Microscopy of Micron-Sized Laser-Written Magnetic Domains in Tbfe." *Appl. Phys. Lett.,* Aug. 1986.

Tlustos, Chris, "Fingerprint ID System Increases Matching Odds." *Government Computer News,* Feb. 14, 1986.

Tomash, Erwin, and Arnold A. Cohen, "The Birth of an ERA: Engineering Research Associates, Inc. 1946-1955." *Annals of the History of Computing,* Oct. 1979.

"Videodiscs and Computers: A Dynamic Duo." *Business Week,* February 7, 1983.

Voelcker, John, "Winchester Disks Reach for a Gigabyte." *IEEE Spectrum,* Feb. 1987.

Waurzyniak, Patrick, "Optical Discs." *InfoWorld,* Dec. 8, 1986.

Welch, Mark J.:
"Big Eight Firm Backs Write-Once Optical Storage." *InfoWorld,* Mar. 24, 1986.
"CD-ROM Arrives." *InfoWorld,* May 26, 1986.

White, Robert M., "Disk-Storage Technology." *Scientific American,* Aug. 1980.

Other Sources

Davies, David H., *"An Optical Disc Primer"* (presentation). Mountain View, Calif.: 3M Corporation, no date.

Geyer, Frederick F., "Thermo-Magneto-Optic Disk Drive in a Systems Environment" (abstract). Sunnyvale, Calif.: Kodak Company, no date.

"The IBM 350 RAMAC Disk File." Santa Clara, Calif.: The American Society of Mechanical Engineers, Feb. 27, 1984.

Lippman, Andrew, "Movie-Maps: An Application of the Optical Videodisc to Computer Graphics" (abstract). 1980 ACM 0-89791-021-4/80/0700-0032.

Majithia, Kenneth, "Optical Storage Subsystems: Promises and Problems" (abstract). San Jose, Calif.: IBM Corporation, no date.

"Optical Disk Pilot Program," by Ellen Z. Hahn, Washington, D.C.: Library of Congress, Oct. 31, 1983.

Acknowledgments

The index for this book was prepared by Mel Ingber. The editors also wish to thank: **In Japan:** Osaka—Matsushita Electrical Industrial Co. Ltd.; Tokyo—Tadashi Watanabe, Nippon Electric Co.; Kazunori Kotani, Nipponcoinco Co. Ltd.; Ricoh Inc.; **In the United States:** Arizona—Tucson: Milburn M. Cochrane and Dan Cost, IBM Corporation; California—Atherton: Philip Rice; Livermore: Sam Coleman, Barbara Costella, and Robert Cralle, Lawrence Livermore National Laboratory; Los Angeles: Darnell Carter and Ruby Nell Samuels, Los Angeles Police Department; Solomon Golomb, University of Southern California; Milpitas: Peter Bischoff and Doug Gerhart, Read-Rite Corporation; Mountain View: Johanna Protsik, Drexler Corporation; David H. Davies and Maria Lashley, 3M Corporation; Palo Alto: Susan Faraone, Karen Kohberger, and Margaret Mehling, Tycer-Fultz-Bellack; Pasadena: Robert J. McEliece, California Institute of Technology; Redwood City: Peter Hammar, Ampex Museum; Sacramento: Elton Johnson, NEC Information Systems; San Diego: James Eggebeen, Data Electronics Inc.; William Bennett, University of California; San Jose: Alan E. Bell, IBM Almaden Research Center; Don Johann and Skip Kilsdonk, Maxtor Corporation; Santa Barbara: Finn Jorgensen, Danvik; Santa Clara: Nathan Ballard, Lin Data Corporation; Scotts Valley: Joan Green, Doug Mahon, and Alan F. Shugart, Seagate Technology; Sunnyvale: Lou Hoffman, Marken Communications; Fred Geyer and Alan Marchant, Verbatim Corporation; Colorado—Broomfield: Data Systems Technology; Colorado Springs: Kim Bayne, Bob Koecheler, David Martin, and Del Miller, Laser Magnetic Storage International; Greeley: Jim Skog, Hewlett-Packard; Longmont: Andrew Hardwick, Miniscribe; Louisville: Samuel D. Cheatham, Steve Haydon, and Cindy Kraybill, Storage Technology; Connecticut—Storrs: Nan Cooper, NERAC, Inc.; Westport: Judith Paris Roth, Optical Information Systems Journal; District of Columbia—John Shore, Entropic Processing, Inc.; Basil Manns, Library of Congress; Marie Mattson and Anne Seeger, Smithsonian Institution; Idaho—Boise: Mike Gordon, Hewlett-Packard; Illinois—Champaign: Ernest Colantio; Maryland—College Park: Eugene Day, University of Maryland; Hunt Valley: Susan Barletta, GeneSys Data Technologies, Inc.; Jessup: William Beck and Maury Kandel, TRW Corporation; Lanham: Neil McElroy, Avelex; John Riganati, Institute for Defense Analyses; Massachusetts—Boston: Gwen Bell, Lynn Hall, and Linda Holecamp, The Computer Museum; Boxborough: Joseph Phillips, NEC Information Systems; Cambridge: Ramon Alonso and Eldon Hall, Draper Labs; Maynard: Stephen A. Kallis, Jr., Digital Equipment Corporation; Shrewsbury: Ed McCarren, Digital Equipment Corporation; Minnesota—Minneapolis: Bruce Bruemmer, Charles Babbage Institute; New Jersey—Princeton: Richard J. Lipton, Princeton University; New York—Albany: Isabel Nirenberg, SUNY Albany; Armonk: John Barton, IBM Corporation; New York: Yoshio Aoki, Sony Corporation; Rochester: Dennis Howe, Eastman Kodak Co.; Valhalla: Donald Kenny, IBM Corporation; White Plains: Mark Root and Ken Croken, IBM Corporation; Yorktown Heights: Karen Appleby, Emerson Pugh, and Mary Van Dusen, IBM Thomas J. Watson Research Lab; Tennessee—Brentwood: Donald Deutsch, General Electric; Virginia—Alexandria: Joe Black, Clinton Computer Systems; Falls Church: Roberta Binder and Rockley Miller, The Videodisc Monitor; Reston: Dennis Fife, George Mason University.

Index

Library of Congress Cataloging in Publication Data

Memory and storage / by the editors of
Time-Life Books.—Rev. ed.
  p. cm. (Understanding computers)
  Includes bibliographical references.
  1. Computer storage devices.
I. Time-Life Books. II. Series.
 TK7895.M4M455 1990   621.39'7—dc20   89-49112 CIP
ISBN 0-8094-7598-7
ISBN 0-8094-7599-5 (lib. bdg.)

For information on and a full description of any Time-Life
Books series, please call 1-800-621-7026 or write:
Reader Information
Time-Life Customer Service
P.O. Box C-32068
Richmond, Virginia 23261-2068

UNDERSTANDING COMPUTERS

SERIES DIRECTOR: Lee Hassig
Series Administrator: Loretta Britten

Editorial Staff for *Memory and Storage*
Designer: Robert K. Herndon
Associate Editors: Allan Fallow (text),
Jeremy Ross (pictures)
Researchers: Steven Feldman, Gregory A. McGruder
Writer: Robert M. S. Somerville
Assistant Designer: Sue Deal
Editorial Assistant: Miriam P. Newton
Picture Coordinator: Renée DeSandies

Special Contributors: Joseph Alper, Ronald H. Bailey,
Elisabeth Carpenter, David Darling, Richard A.
Jenkins, Martin Mann, John I. Merritt, Steve Olson, Jim
Watson (text); Robert M. McDowell, Carol Nicotera,
Sally Vandershaf, Marlene Zimmerman (research);
Jayne E. Rohrich (copyediting).

Correspondents: Elisabeth Kraemer-Singh (Bonn);
Maria Vincenza Aloisi (Paris); Ann Natanson (Rome).
Valuable assistance was also provided by: Elizabeth
Brown and Christina Lieberman (New York); Dick
Berry (Tokyo).

CONSULTANTS

WILLIAM E. BURR is manager, Advanced Communications Group, Institute for Computer Sciences and Technology, National Bureau of Standards.

NEAL GLOVER of Data Systems Technology Corp., is a leading expert on the practical application of error-correction codes. He holds several patents in the field of error-detection and -correction and is the author of the book *Practical Error Correction Design for Engineers.*

BRIAN HAYES has written about computers and computing for such periodicals as *Scientific American, BYTE,* and *Computer Language.* He is author of a book about Scheme, a dialect of the LISP programming language.

ALBERT S. HOAGLAND is director of the Institute for Information Storage Technology at Santa Clara University. He made major contributions to magnetic recording technology during twenty-eight years at IBM and is the author of *Digital Magnetic Recording.*

MICHAEL D. HOGAN is manager of the Storage Media Group at the National Bureau of Standards. Since joining the Bureau in 1977, he has worked on developing standards for rigid and flexible magnetic disks.

LEONARD LAUB is the president and founder of Vision Three, Inc., a New York consulting firm that specializes in computer and information-management businesses. He has been active in the development and commercialization of optical disks since the mid-1960s.

JONAH MCLEOD is associate managing editor of *Electronics* magazine. He is the author of *Winchester Disks in Microcomputer Systems* and an optical-storage report for Electronic Trend Publishing.

MICHAEL R. WILLIAMS, a professor of computer science at the University of Calgary in Canada, is the author of *A History of Computing Technology.*